D1220021

Michael Haneke

Contemporary Film Directors

Edited by James Naremore

The Contemporary Film Directors series provides concise, well-written introductions to directors from around the world and from every level of the film industry. Its chief aims are to broaden our awareness of important artists, to give serious critical attention to their work, and to illustrate the variety and vitality of contemporary cinema. Contributors to the series include an array of internationally respected critics and academics. Each volume contains an incisive critical commentary, an informative interview with the director, and a detailed filmography.

A list of books in the series appears at the end of this book.

Michael Haneke |

Peter Brunette

**UNIVERSITY
OF
ILLINOIS
PRESS**
URBANA
AND
CHICAGO

Frontispiece: Michael Haneke.

Library of Congress Cataloging-in-Publication Data
Brunette, Peter.
Michael Haneke / Peter Brunette.
p.   cm. — (Contemporary film directors)
Includes bibliographical references and index.
ISBN 978-0-252-03531-9 (cloth : alk. paper)
ISBN 978-0-252-07717-3 (pbk. : alk. paper)
1. Haneke, Michael, 1942—Criticism and interpretation.
I. Title.
PN1998.3.H36B78   2010
791.43023'3092—dc22   2009037098

To my sister Rose, who rescued me, at least twice,
And to the memory of Lynne Johnson, my wife.

Contents |

Acknowledgments

I want to thank Roy Grundmann and especially Jim Naremore, the editor of the series in which this book appears and my friend of forty years, for their astute readings of an earlier version of the manuscript. Their suggestions have caused me to think more deeply about Haneke than I ever would have been able to on my own. Responsibility for factual errors and misreadings that remain, of course, lies solely with me. My Wake Forest colleagues and friends, David Lubin and Dick Schneider, have provided endless intellectual stimulation in the five years I have known them, and I am deeply grateful for their friendship and continued support. I also want to thank Gary Palmucci of Kino International for all his help with various and sundry things, and my technology guru in the art department at Wake Forest, Paul Marley, for assistance with photographs.

Michael Haneke |

Violence, Representation, Responsibility

The Films of Michael Haneke

You never show reality; you only show its manipulated image.
—Michael Haneke

Introduction

Michael Haneke burst out of the festival ghetto onto the international art-house scene in 2005 with his challenging and (to some) distressingly open-ended French-language film *Caché* (Hidden), and he solidified his position as a major contemporary auteur by winning the Palme d'Or at the Cannes Film Festival in 2009. He is a provocative figure who likes to disturb people, most notably his audiences.

The overarching themes that unite Haneke's films are not especially novel: the alienation from self and others that contemporary society routinely produces, the attendant loss of our common humanity (what he has called "our social and psychological wound"), the grinding attenuation of human emotion, the increasingly elaborate systems of communication that manage to communicate less and less, and the relationship between reality and its representation. These are themes that have been around at least since the 1960s, in the films of the Italian master Michelangelo

Antonioni, among others, but they have been brilliantly updated through the application of fresh and even iconoclastic cinematic techniques by this surprisingly old-school art-film director.

Partly because these general themes are so familiar, one aspect of Haneke's films that has garnered a great deal of attention throughout the latter part of his career has been the "subtheme" of the specific role of contemporary media in producing such social alienation. Most important of all, however, has been his complex and multifaceted exploration of violence. At his press conference at Cannes in May 2009, Haneke baldly stated, "All my films are about violence." Though it takes a different form each time, probably the most controversial aspect of this ongoing investigation has concerned what Haneke considers the "consumable" way in which violence is represented in Hollywood movies. In this arena, he has consistently challenged critics and film viewers, in the name of art, to consider their own responsibility for what they watch and to ask themselves just what it is they are *really* doing when they seek to be "merely" entertained by a studio-produced Hollywood thriller.

This has placed Haneke in a somewhat anomalous position, for many of his films are too intellectual and self-consciously avant-garde to attract his presumed target audience (those viewers who actually watch violent thrillers), yet simultaneously too graphic and upsetting to please the majority of the art-film crowd—those looking for something "life-affirming," preferably in a foreign language with English words on the bottom of the screen. And then there is the radicality of his formal means, including a purposely fragmented and confusing narrative and a liberal use of the long-take in which "nothing happens," as the proverbial criticism of this powerful, if demanding, aesthetic would have it.

Haneke, now approaching seventy, is an extremely well-read European intellectual who originally came from the theater and who has also been trained in and profoundly influenced by classical music. Many critics have taken up this latter aspect of his films in some detail (see especially Frey, "Cinema," "Supermodernity"; Vicari; Grundmann); however, owing to space constraints and the lack of the requisite expertise on the part of the present writer, this study will largely pass over the fascinating musical connections that obtain in his films. Rather, it will concern itself with an elaboration of the director's recurring themes in light of his formal cinematic techniques, primarily those that are visual or (nonmusically) aural.

Michael Haneke was born in 1942. His career is something of an anomaly, since he had worked in Austrian and German television for nearly two decades before making his first feature film, *The Seventh Continent* (Der siebente Kontinent, 1989), for theatrical release. He has since made eight or nine (depending on how you count them) highly distinctive theatrical films that long ago captured the attention of festival-going critics around the world but have only relatively recently come to the attention of the larger art-film public, especially the most recent French-language productions starring Isabelle Huppert and Juliette Binoche. It is these films that this book will focus upon.

The earlier, quite fascinating, and only recently unearthed television films—which, alas, are too numerous and too scarce to examine closely here—often present themselves, surprisingly, in the guise of somewhat old-fashioned modernist experimentation. In their formal rigor, frank themes, and general harshness of tone, they are the polar opposite of what in the United States would generally be considered a "television film."[1] The full frontal female nudity and the self-consciously, resolutely downbeat Weltanschauung unashamedly expressed in these nearly thirty-year-old television productions underscore the vast gulf that has always separated much European television from its unrecognizable American cousin. In terms of Haneke's career, what is important to keep in mind, as he told the American critic Scott Foundas, was that for him working in television "was not a matter of not having the opportunity to make a real film. But rather, I wanted to find my own language."

The other noteworthy element in these early films (which have never been commercially released in any country or format) is a bitter, ongoing sociopolitical critique of the middle class, a beloved target of most German-speaking artists but especially, it sometimes seems, those from Austria. His masterpiece of this period, the two-part *Lemmings* (Lemminge, 1979), is a brilliant, full-scale assault on bourgeois pieties, yet its critique is also historically specific and attempts to account for the spiritual emptiness of the generation—Haneke's own—whose parents' lives were defined by the exigencies of World War II and Nazism. (He has returned to this generational, sociohistorical vein in *The White Ribbon*

[Das Weisse Band, 2009], which takes place just before the outbreak of World War I.) Unfortunately, what is also occasionally on display in this film, which is set in 1959 (part I) and 1979 (part II), is the less palatable side of the director's work and personality that occasionally comes into view: the hectoring scold and unassailable moral arbiter.

It is probably a mistake to try to analyze Haneke's work of any period solely in terms of the aesthetic protocols of international art-film production. Rather, the profound, never fully explained unhappiness that engulfs many of his characters—in the television work and the later films—is best understood in relation to the irrational violence and profound malaise infecting the fictional characters of his countrywoman, the Nobel Prize–winning writer Elfriede Jelinek, and other cinematic figures, like the younger filmmaker Ulrich Seidl (*Dog Days*, 2001; *Import/Export*, 2007), both of whom also concentrate on horribly lost souls who seem to have no overt rationale for the ultra-intensity of their frustration, violence, and inhumanity.

At least some of this bitterness may be traced to Austria's particular relationship to the events before, during, and after World War II, especially regarding the never-resolved, little-examined dalliance with the Nazi party and Adolf Hitler, who was born in Austria. Other countries, like France and Italy, have had their own postwar devils to wrestle with, in terms of the elaborate discourses of "victimhood" that have had to be generated, retrospectively, by each society, but Austria has had particular difficulty justifying its warm embrace of the Nazi Anschluss of 1938 while also claiming bragging rights as Hitler's "first victims." As Haneke himself has said, "In Austria today you still hear people proclaim that 'None of us were Nazis.' No one will admit to being a Nazi; they were all victims of the Nazis" (Porton 50).

In addition, the Austrian population and military suffered much more immediately and severely than the French, who in effect dropped out of the war within a few months. We see the psychological scars of this suffering, and of the refusal to confront the compromised past, in the work of Haneke and Jelinek and, at a further remove, Seidl and other younger figures. (The autobiographical element has also to be taken into account in trying to understand a film like *Lemmings*, given the fact that the characters who populate the film are the same age and live in the same town as the director who created them.)

With his theatrical films, beginning with *The Seventh Continent* (1989), Haneke switches gears. His general social critique about the inhumanity of modern life is still paramount, but what now comes more fully into view is a particular feature of that critique, his ongoing exploration of the cinematic and televisual representation of violence—a critique that is itself sometimes expressed in a violent fashion. A family destroys all their possessions and then themselves, graphically, in *The Seventh Continent*. In *Benny's Video*, a teenager from a cosseted bourgeois family kills a young girl he's recently met with a bolt gun used to slaughter hogs, while capturing the action on video. The psychological pressures that lead a military cadet to kill four people in a bank are explored in *71 Fragments of a Chronology of Chance*, while *Funny Games* presents two young men who torture and eventually murder a father, mother, and their young son. In the later French-language films, Haneke moves away from this focus on violence and its representation in the media toward a more generalized critique of contemporary, especially urban, life. *The White Ribbon* applies the same critique, but this time to an historical period a century in the past.

The films that focus on the representation of violence, however, raise a perhaps unintended moral question: To what extent do these films also *participate* in the "pleasures" of the violence they ostensibly critique? An earlier model would be Stanley Kubrick's *A Clockwork Orange* (1971), which, intentionally antiviolence, has been thought by many critics to revel in its very graphic depictions of violence.

It is perhaps appropriate here to cite some of the things that Haneke and others have said on this subject, though the question will also be considered on a film-by-film basis throughout this book. One camp wants to absolve Haneke of any responsibility. Christopher Sharrett has said that one of Haneke's most notorious films, *Funny Games* (1997), does not "participate, for all its relentlessness, in the excesses it criticizes," though such an arbitrary boundary is difficult to establish. The critic Scott Foundas says that movies like *Funny Games* and *Benny's Video* "are graphic and intense, but Haneke doesn't (as his detractors would claim) profit from their violence. Rather, he reclaims sensitivity to violence (and to human suffering) from the exploitative wastelands of Jerrys, Bruckheimer and Springer." Others, however, like the *New York Times* critic A. O. Scott, speaking of the failed 2007 American remake of *Funny Games*, has called Haneke a "fraud" who tortures not only his characters but his audience as well.

By way of self-explanation, Haneke has said that "the society we live in is drenched in violence. I represent it on the screen because I am afraid of it, and I think it is important that we should reflect on it. . . . I think that the things that are going well in society are difficult to present dramatically. In my 20 years of working in the theater, I only staged one comedy, and that was my single failure" (Badt).

Haneke's focus, in other words, is on the ubiquitous presence of violence in the real world and the representation of such violence in the media. For obvious reasons, the latter is more sharply foregrounded in his films, since they are inevitably part of that media. Representation is always about "showing," and thus the question that inevitably arises is what can and cannot legitimately be shown, or "re-presented." Asked by Foundas how he is able to treat sensational subjects in what Foundas describes as "a non-sensational manner," the director's surprisingly moralistic reply is that while he respects the gravity of these events, a lot of Hollywood films simply exploit them. "For example, if you take *Schindler's List* and you have that shower scene, I think it's absolutely disgusting to show that. One must not show such things."

Instead, Haneke chooses to keep most violence offscreen: "I use your fantasy. I think it's one of the most important things for a filmmaker. . . . The audience has to make their pictures, and whatever I show means diminishing the fantasy of the viewer" (Foundas). The fact that most of the brutality in the director's films is offscreen is also used by his devotees to exonerate Haneke of any moral failing in this regard. But just because violence is not actually *pictured*, it is nevertheless always *heard*, and its aftermath is seen, and thus it is always directly represented in his films in some complex way that goes beyond the visual.

Haneke also knows that the question is more complex than merely showing or not showing violence onscreen.

> I'm trying as best I can to describe a situation as I see it without bullshit-ting or disingenuousness, but by so doing I subscribe to the notion that communication is still possible, otherwise I wouldn't be doing

this. I cannot make comedies about these subjects, so it is true the films are bleak.

The new technologies, of both media representation and the political world, allow greater damage with ever-increasing speed. The media contribute to a confused consciousness through this illusion that we know all things at all times, and always with this great sense of immediacy. We live in this environment where we think we know more things faster, when in fact we know nothing at all. This propels us into terrible internal conflicts, which then creates angst, which in turn causes aggression, and this creates violence. This is a vicious cycle. (Sharrett)

And whence comes Haneke's obsession with violence and its representation, when so many other directors are content to exploit it ruthlessly? "I think that I am someone who is creative, and sensitive to every form of suffering," the director says, in an interview translated for this volume. "That makes me think of Wim Wenders's film *The End of Violence*, which begins by trying to define violence. I myself have asked that question, and the answer that I found is that violence is the ultimate recourse of power against the will of others who must then be subjected to it." This definition of violence is especially applicable to *The White Ribbon*.

Presiding over Haneke's aesthetics is the notion that films can be art and that true art requires a contract with the audience. Mainstream cinema, on the contrary, emphasizes "the commercial aspects of the medium. . . . I think what I'm proposing is a very old contractual agreement—that both the producer and receiver of a work of art take each other seriously. On the other hand, today's conventional cinema, or mass cinema . . . sees the audience member as a bank machine, whose only function is to spit out money. It pretends to satisfy viewers' needs, but refuses to do so" (Porton 51). Above all, Haneke feels that audience members must be persuaded—or forced, if necessary—to contribute to a film's meaning themselves and to recognize their complicity in its psychological dynamics. It is here that the director's aesthetic mission sometimes comes perilously close to aesthetic coercion.

The director's formal techniques, especially in the earliest films of the "theatrical" period, are complex and invigorating but simultaneously difficult and off-putting to those with little experience with art films. Interestingly, his use of techniques that might in another context be called postmodernist is anything but, for much of the motivation for his trans-gressive subject matter and his distancing techniques is modernist to the core. This modernism is linked tightly to a now rather hoary concept of art, which, like the word "truth," is never far from his lips. Both mark him as something of a throwback to an earlier generation, or perhaps a younger member of the modernist group of directors that includes canonical fig-ures like Antonioni, Resnais, Godard, Bergman, and Tarkovsky.

Formal techniques, for Haneke, also carry a philosophical rationale. If he sometimes maddeningly refuses to explain character motivation in a conventional manner, for example, it's because "every kind of explanation is just something that's there to make you feel better, and at the same time it's a lie. It's a lie to calm you, because the real explanation would be so complex, it would be impossible to have in 90 minutes of film or 200 pages of a novel" (Foundas).

Similarly, many of his films rely upon a series of vignettes, fragments that cut to black and often resist synthesis at a higher level. Again, the result is a kind of counter-cinema that defies commercial considerations. According to Haneke, films can never, by definition, show reality as a whole, so fragmentation is the only honest way to proceed. One must then "find the aesthetic means that will allow us to transfer this frag-mented look onto the screen" (Cieutat interview in this volume).

The fragments themselves often consist of a single long-take (with the camera either stationary or panning to follow the characters), a tech-nique, originally championed by the celebrated French critic and theo-rist André Bazin, that is notoriously bothersome to the generation raised on the jumpy editing of MTV—and not only to them. This technique represents an attempt to fashion a counter-cinema that would oppose not only Hollywood filmmaking but its nefarious ally, television, with which, having begun there, Haneke has a paradoxical relationship:

> Perhaps I can connect [the long-take] to the issue of television. Televi-sion accelerates our habits of seeing. Look, for example, at advertising in that medium. The faster something is shown, the less able you are to perceive it as an object occupying a space in physical reality and the more it becomes something seductive. And the less real the image seems to be, the quicker you buy the commodity it seems to depict.

Of course, this type of aesthetic has gained the upper hand in commercial cinema. Television accelerates experience, but one needs time to understand what one sees, which the current media disallows. Not just understand on an intellectual level, but emotionally. The cinema can offer very little that is new; everything that is said has been said a thousand times, but cinema still has the capacity, I think, to let us experience the world anew. (Sharrett)

This capacity to reexperience the world is thus reinvigorated by the long-take aesthetic. *"Code inconnu [Code Unknown,* Haneke's first French-language film, released in 2000] consists very much of static sequences, with each shot from only one perspective, precisely because I don't want to patronize or manipulate the viewer, or at least to the smallest degree possible" (Sharrett).

Nor is Haneke naive regarding the question of manipulation, a subject that always entails rethinking the role of the audience, though he does seem to believe that manipulation can be quantified: "Of course, film is always manipulation, but if each scene is only one shot, then, I think, there is at least less of a sense of *time* being manipulated when one tries to stay close to a 'real time' framework. The reduction of montage to a minimum also tends to shift responsibility back to the viewer in that contemplation is required" (Sharrett).[2]

But if even the most careful cinema is always manipulative, why bother? What kind of solution to the world's problems can filmmakers hope to provide? "The point is that there are no solutions," Haneke bleakly insists.

The mainstream cinema tries to feed you the idea that there are solutions, but that's bullshit. You can make a lot of money with these lies. But if you take the viewer seriously as your partner, the only thing that you can do is to put the questions strongly. In this case, maybe he will find some answer. If you give the answer, you lie. Whatever kind of security you try to feed somebody is an illusion. . . . I want to make it clear: it's not that I hate mainstream cinema. It's perfectly fine. There are a lot of people who need to escape, because they are in very difficult situations. . . . But this has nothing to do with an art form. An art form is obliged to confront reality, to try to find a little piece of the truth. . . . These questions, "What is reality?" and "What is reality in a movie?" are a main part of my work. (Foundas)

An essential part of this confrontation with reality necessarily entails the self-exploration of the artist—some of it, notably in *Funny Games*, of a self-reflexive variety. It is precisely this gesture, according to Haneke, that leads us back to art, because, to be considered an art form, film must challenge its own existence: "The question is, is film merely entertainment, or is it more? If it is art, it has to be more. Art can be entertaining. *The Passion of St. Matthew* is entertaining, [but] it is more than diversion, it is concentration, [it] focuses your thoughts" So cinema can change the world? "No, but it can make it a less sad place than it already is" (Badt).

The Seventh Continent (1989)

In his first feature-length film made for theatrical distribution, Michael Haneke clearly enunciates the uncompromising, sometimes bitter critique of contemporary society that will mark all of his films to come. The rigorous formal technique that makes little or no allowance for popular taste is also fully present in the obsessive attention to framing, composition, color, and editing—as opposed to more conventional dramatic ele-

Figure 1. Birgit Doll and Dieter Berner prepare for a take in *The Seventh Continent*.

ments, like plot, character, and dialogue—and in the sounds, sometimes harsh and sometimes falsely soothing, that fill our everyday lives.

As is well known by anyone who has seen his films, or even read about them, Haneke's critique of modern society often takes the form of an exploration of violence and its representation in the media. In this first film, however, the violence—excluding that central, outrageous, and inescapable violence of a family committing collective suicide—seems mostly limited to that unspectacular variety that works on us subconsciously, according to Haneke, in our everyday lives.

The Seventh Continent, like virtually all of the director's films, concentrates on middle-class family life (following his model, Antonioni, he has said that this is what he knows, hence what he makes films about), though here the focus is obsessively on one particular family who, without any overt thought or discussion that Haneke chooses to represent (since, according to him, it can never be known), decide to destroy all of their property and themselves. It is a film, and a story, so relentless in its approach, and so egregious, that it would be hard to bear and even harder to credit—literally *in-credible*—if we did not know beforehand that it is based on an event that Haneke had read about in a newspaper.

Georg, Anna, and their little daughter Evi seem to have the perfect bourgeois life. (These are the names that Haneke gives the central characters in virtually all his films, as if to emphasize a kind of Eisensteinian "typage" rather than a specificity of individualized character that doesn't really interest him.) Their days are filled with the shiny objects and routine duties that define our contemporary existence in the developed world, and as Haneke takes pains to point out in the interview with Serge Toubiana included on the Kino Films DVD, it's an existence that is in no way intended to be limited to present-day Austria, where the film is ostensibly set. They are meant to be typical, and they represent "the" family rather than any specific family.

According to the Toubiana interview, Haneke originally conceived of the structure of the film as a series of flashbacks from the point of view of the moribund Georg, who has just ingested a handful of pills, but the director couldn't make it work. Then he hit upon the idea of showing three different days in the life of the family, in 1987, 1988, and 1989, and this frame functioned so well that he was able to write the entire screenplay in four weeks. Clearly, the choice of this particular structure further accentuates the "typicality" of what we see over the course of the three days. Each day is a kind of synecdoche for an entire year, and the three days put together form the history of a family.

Haneke's uncompromising decision to tell his story primarily through visual means and sound effects, rather than with dialogue, dramatic action, or conventional character studies, is apparent from the first, even during the credit sequence. We realize immediately that we have entered a hyper-Hitchcockian world in which virtually everything that we see and hear has been explicitly chosen by the filmmaker and his collaborators. It is the essence of what has been called "closed form": graphic design is heavily foregrounded, though we are torn, perhaps, between finding the particular visual design of this film pleasing or alienating. Its effect is always immensely cold and seems, in its opening moments and throughout the film, the purposefully chosen antithesis of the warm, wet viscera of what was once considered the essence of human life. Consequently, his own composition, like the objects found within it, is both visually compelling and utterly frigid (whence the label "the glaciation trilogy," which Haneke himself disdains, for this and the two subsequent films).

The images in the car wash (a repetitive motif in the film) are, in a manner of speaking, violent from the first, in the harsh sounds produced by the mechanism itself and in the alienating blasts from the soaping agent and the brushes. The family is undertaking that most bourgeois of tasks—the cleansing ritual of washing the family car—and are protected from the artificial constructions that rage around them, if also isolated by the metal frame they inhabit and that seems to hold them frozen in place. (We can tell by the license plate that the story takes place in Linz, a medium-sized city in Austria, but Haneke has said in the Toubiana interview that nothing was shot in that city. There are no other references in the film to it nor to any other place, in Austria or elsewhere.)

The harshness of the mechanical cleansing seems to stand against anything that could be construed as pertaining to the vulnerable viscerality of human bodies. The static, artificial, perfectly balanced framing, along with the family's expressionless faces, conveys an impression of death-in-life. When they drive out of the car wash, the car now all clean and shiny, they pass a "Welcome to Australia" billboard, which shows a beach, the sea, and a mountain, with "Australian Travel Agency" written in the lower left-hand corner. A version of this poster (minus the writing but with the sea moving, accompanied by the appropriate, apparently nondiegetic sound effects) will become a major motif in the film, appearing several more times. For Haneke, the image is "calm, but it's a frightening calmness. [Later on] it could be their memory of that image that they saw when washing the car. An image that has become upsetting for them, or an image of peace. It's ambiguous" (Toubiana interview). Australia seems to reflect the "seventh continent" of the film's title, the "place" to which the family is emigrating, as they explain at one point in a letter, when in fact they have actually chosen the lost continent of destruction and death.

Part I (1987) begins, and from this point forward, the story will be told in a series of vignettes, some quite short, others much longer, that always end with a cut to black that is held relatively—some might say pretentiously—long. Haneke told Michel Cieutat, in an interview that is included in this volume, that the "black shots" were intended to "create a real sense of fragmentation. [In this film], their duration corresponded to the depth of the preceding scene. If there was a lot to think about in the sequence, I made the black last longer." It's an open question, of course, whether viewers, while watching a black screen, actually spend this time contemplating the previous image or impatiently awaiting the next.

Interestingly, when Haneke does feel the occasional need to provide some modicum of narrative logic or character motivation, it is almost always via a highly conventional narrative device, the letters that Anna or Georg write to Georg's parents, which we hear read aloud in voiceover. Another device that feints in the direction of a revelation of character psychology, though it (purposely) doesn't deliver, involves close-ups of their daughter Evi. In several of the more extended scenes—for example, the scene in which Georg sells the family car—the camera relentlessly cuts, over and over, to a (usually blank) reaction shot on Evi, as though filtering events, by implication, through her consciousness or her perspective might make them more primitive and, because of her innocence, even more violently invasive.

Most provocatively, the opening vignettes either focus on the manufactured objects (usually extremely colorful, shiny, and new) that provide the context for their lives or on various parts of the family members' bodies—never their faces or their entire bodies—which are almost always covered by clothing. As Haneke explained it to Toubiana, "Only pieces are shown in the beginning to show how we are . . . dominated by serving daily life. They don't live; they do things. They repeat gestures. We're stuck with these gestures, and our whole life is the sum total of these gestures. . . . [Then] they destroy everything in their lives with the same methodical obsessiveness. . . . That could be an act of liberation, but the way they do it shows that it's not a liberation for them, and for me, that's the saddest part of the film. We could have made a provocative film, from the middle forward, as an act of liberation. But to me, that would have been a lie."

What reigns above all is *detail*. The alarm clock in the parents' bedroom shows 6:00 A.M., and the news starts immediately, indicating again an inhuman, mechanical precision of synchronicity. The orange and blue colors that predominate are creepily artificial yet complementary and beautiful at the same time. The garage door opens, the car moves out as if driven by a robot, and the garage door closes once again. Several shots of Georg's workplace—with its industrial equipment outside and the huge bank of ceiling lights over an empty space inside—will remind viewers of Antonioni's *Red Desert*, that earlier, equally ambiguous critique of modern technological alienation.

At times, a kind of falsely soothing Muzak can be heard on the soundtrack, especially when the family members, in the supermarket, are being encouraged by an anonymous voice to consume more products. Mostly, however, mechanical, jarring sounds reign supreme, and the quintessential object (which we see in many different forms throughout the film) becomes the adding machine or cash register—simultaneously visually imposing objects (especially photographed, as they almost always are, in extreme close-up) and the source of powerful and disturbing noises. Primarily, they are objects designed to reduce human interaction to its economic or numerical dimension. Rarely, if ever, do we see natural objects such as trees or even something as normally ubiquitous as grass.

No faces are shown for an inordinately long period, a technique that graphically demonstrates Haneke's contention that objects have triumphed over people and, at the same time, keeps us from identifying with them as "real people," or characters with whom we might establish an emotional bond. Later on, when faces *are* shown, we almost always see them in artificial, strongly lighted portraitlike poses against neutral backgrounds, which further emphasize their rigid, nonhuman quality.

Haneke's themes are not difficult to divine. It's clear that he has a point to make, and he has no intention of using a worn-out, perhaps even complicitous realism to make it. Thus it might be objected that presumably there are *some* happy moments in everyone's life, but Haneke has chosen to show us little or nothing of that here. And since his intention seems to be to make a philosophical point about contemporary life, it doesn't matter how far the depicted events stray from versimilitude, especially since it is precisely the tyranny of the "everyday," as he suggests in the Toubiana interview, that is his target.

In any case, his goal seems to be to go beyond a banal, overly familiar critique of first-world consumerism to attack, on an almost metaphysical level (in the technical sense of that word, as the philosophy of *being*), the very status of manufactured objects in our lives. But, as is typical for a Haneke film, it is impossible to assign specific meanings, especially since he tells Toubiana that "I tried to tell this story without giving any answers" and, in the same interview, roundly criticizes the journalist for attempting to fill in all the explanations in the newspaper story that originally inspired the director: "He had debts, he couldn't pay, he had sexual problems with his wife, et cetera. All these stupid explanations diminished the power of the gesture." Haneke continues: "Nobody writing a novel would want to write something that claimed to understand everything that happens in the story. It's the same with film. If you want to explain something, it can only be explained through structure. . . . But it's always ambiguous, as opposed to narrating in a way that is always trying to explain. It's too talky and banal that way." Precisely what Haneke means by "structure" here is itself ambiguous, but it seems to point to an aesthetic construction that goes beyond the explanatory power of words that necessarily always oversimplify. In any case, the complexity of this formulation indicates that Haneke has thought deeply, in this film and elsewhere, about exactly what he is trying to do, whether or not he lets his audience in on the secret.

Soon after the beginning of the film, the juxtaposition of the mechanical and the visceral is pointedly reinforced. Anna is part-owner, with her brother, of a shop that sells eyeglasses, and she is in the midst of performing an eye examination on an older woman, who nonchalantly tells a story about cruelty inflicted upon a classmate many decades earlier. This motif of *seeing* (always complemented by a hyperactive sound track) also ties in with what might be called the very first narrative episode of the film, in which Evi, for no good reason and to the consternation of her teacher and her mother, pretends to be blind.

Throughout the sequence of the eye examination, we are forced to watch the woman's eyeball in extreme close-up, rather than in the more usual context of her face, and thus paradoxically the effect is to dehumanize her eyes by decontextualizing them—by removing them from her face, via the optometry equipment and the camera. Yet the palpitating actions of the iris and the sight of various throbbing blood vessels, on infinitely closer display than we ever encounter them in real life, also stand in severe contrast to the machine that is being used to examine them.

Many short sequences seem to be almost random, purposely banal reports on the living of daily life, while others last longer and have more dramatic force, such as the dinner scene, which includes the immediate family and Anna's brother. The unnatural, highly theatrical lighting and detached, stationary camera position create, once again, a purposely artificial and antihuman effect. Social conventions rule, as always, over human needs, and when Anna's brother finally breaks down and begins sobbing over the recent death of their mother, it seems to take forever for Anna to move closer to solace him.

Later, Anna also breaks down in a moving, though quieter scene (which ends part II), once again in the car wash, but Haneke offers no apparent explanation for her sadness at this point. It's as though the sheer weight of life, especially the daily mechanical grind of contemporary life, simply overwhelms her. Once again, while these humans are "protected" inside their machines, they have to become almost machines themselves to remain "safe." What's different this time around is that Anna reaches her hand back to hold Evi's, then releases it, while her husband gently touches Anna's face, though without asking her why she is crying. The final shot before going to black is of Evi's hands anxiously clasping each other.

After the dinner scene discussed above, the family members sit and watch television and are completely enveloped by its ethereal yet deathly blue light. It is here that Haneke's specific critique of the media (hinted at throughout via the constant stream of bad news on the radio) begins to develop in a fledgling way that will be greatly expanded upon in subsequent films. What they watch seems to be a program on Swiss television, in which a female "presenter" is talking in a mélange of English, French, and German, suggesting a Babel of words but little genuine human communication, an important Hanekean topos. To complicate these linguistic matters, a television voiceover repeats the English and French parts in German for the Austrian audience—and, of course, non-German-speaking viewers of Haneke's film are simultaneously reading the film's subtitles in English or some other language.

At this point, Anna's brother makes the cryptic comment, "Mom said a few days before dying: 'Sometimes I wonder what it would be like if we had a monitor instead of a head where we could see our thoughts.'" This bit of dialogue, which seems intended as an indictment of the "mediatization" of all that is viscerally human (and which accords well with the critique of mechanization and objectification), obviously correlates with the vision/visual theme developed through the eye examination. It also ties in with Evi's faked blindness in school (for which she is brutally slapped by her mother, despite her promise not to punish Evi if she tells the truth) and a newspaper story about a little girl that we glimpse later, whose headline reads "Blind—but Never Again Alone," while the accompanying subhead partially explains, "After a Horrible Accident, Anita Can Count on the Affection of Her Parents. More Than Before." A cinematic technique related to this motif of seeing/not seeing involves the preponderance of "unanswered" eyeline matches in the film, as when Evi looks up toward a place that her mother is probably occupying, yet we don't see the mother in a reverse-angle shot that would logically "complete" the sequence.

Part II (1988) starts just a few minutes before part I began, but a year later, as we witness Anna and Georg making love. There is a lot of heavy breathing, but no talking. The radio alarm goes off at precisely 6:00 A.M. and, just like a year earlier, the radio news starts. Husband and wife exchange "good mornings," then all of the petty details of everyday morning life are shown almost exactly as they were in 1987—the slippers, gathering up sheets, picking up bathrobe, opening bedroom door—though now the three toothbrushes that are lined up in the bathroom with military precision are different colors than before, indicating both the passage of time and the sameness that rules their lives. One thing in part II doesn't quite fit, however, and that's a scene of Anna in a doctor's waiting room; only later, in part III, when she's there again, do we realize that she is gathering the medications they will use to kill themselves. (This later knowledge also presumably explains, in retrospect, why Anna sobs in the car wash at the end of part II.)

Another powerful, if understated dramatic scene comes when an old man, whom Georg is replacing as head of the department, comes in to pick up his personal belongings. We sympathize with him, and Georg appears to as well. The genuine affect of the moment contrasts strongly with the selfishness of the views expressed about the same situation in Anna's letter to Georg's parents that we have just heard in voiceover. It's as though the very structure of modern life—and not necessarily capitalism itself, for Haneke is never a narrowly "political" filmmaker—creates the ground for a cruelty that might otherwise not be there, if human relations could be allowed to retain their primordial human content.

An even more visually striking moment, now completely wordless, comes when the family, once again "safely" ensconced in their car, encounters an accident scene that temporarily, and to their annoyance, slows them down. The bodies they pass are heaped up under a large piece of plastic that lets us guess what they are but never shows us anything actually human. The viscera are once again hidden away, as Haneke demonstrates his mastery at revealing and hiding at the same time.

In part III (1989) we are inundated with close-ups of the family leaving Georg's parents' house, without ever having seen anything of their stay there. Strangely, we again see only objects and body parts, no faces, as at the beginning of the film, until we are finally granted a shot of the grandfather's face—is it too obvious that he stands in front of a wall of organic wood shingles rather than the manufactured plastic and metal objects we see everywhere else?—as the grandmother moves into the frame, and both wave goodbye.

The first overt sign that something seriously untoward is about to occur is Georg's announcement that the newspaper subscription should be canceled. (Haneke has avoided any attempt at open foreshadowing, though he does include situations that we can only understand retrospectively, like Anna's visits to the doctor and the sobbing in the car wash, presumably counting on us to realize that, given this environment, something awful is eventually bound to happen.) In the voiceover reading of a letter to the grandparents—for once, in Georg's voice—we hear about a "decision" that has been taken. In the next several scenes, Haneke works a clever ambiguity concerning the meaning of their decision to "emigrate" to a different location. We still have no idea exactly what is going to happen, but given the general somberness of tone, we fear the worst.

The scenes of abject destruction that ensue are surely unequaled in film history and reflect the same obsessive sense of detail that dominated parts I and II. Even the tools that will be used to destroy their apartment and all its contents seem particularly bright and shiny. Haneke points out in the interview with Toubiana that two scenes especially disturbed the audiences who first saw the film at its premiere at Cannes. The first was the one in which the aquarium is destroyed (despite Anna crying out "no!" just before Georg wields the axe), with the attendant horrifying images of flopping, dying fish. The second was the scene in which the family, after withdrawing their life savings from the bank, assiduously, and at great length, flushes all the money down the toilet. As Haneke tells Toubiana, "It's much less upsetting to show parents killing their children than to show money being destroyed. It's a total taboo in our society. The real people did this—I don't know whether I could have made it up!"

While Evi works on her coloring book, Georg, in his voiceover reading of the letter to his parents, tells them of the debate about whether they should take her with them or leave her with Granny and Grandpa. After speaking of Evi's assent to the words of a cantata the family has heard in church, "I look forward to my death," he says to his parents, abstractly but firmly, "I believe that looking at the life we have lived straight in the eye makes any notion of the end easy to accept. Please don't be sad, or reproach yourselves with the situation, or consider it as a form of critique or whatever; I am only making a statement of fact, which has nothing to do with you."

We next see the three enjoying the fancy meal they have had catered, while, for virtually the first time in the film, they offer delicate smiles to each other as they chew away at their food (a favorite Haneke image in this film, and possibly intended as a reminder of the visceral humanity that inevitably accompanies all human images, especially of the face).

Figure 2. Anna (Birgit Doll), Georg (Dieter Berner), and Eva (Leni Tanzer) enjoy their last meal in *The Seventh Continent*.

The next morning, a lovely breakfast is produced, a scene that is crosscut in perfect, relentless harmony with the preparation of the tools of destruction. Here Haneke, through the mechanical precision of his editing, almost seems to abet or echo Georg's sick idea, just after beginning his nasty work, that "we can only do this if we do it systematically."

The colors of the destroying and the destroyed objects continue to be ultravibrant—for example, the bright blue gloves being worn to tear up the gold-yellow sweater. The actions are rigorous and crisp, and in that, they parallel the earlier (albeit more peaceful) activities of their everyday lives. A definite, powerful rhythm accompanies the destruction, as we move from shirts ripped up by hand to chain saws cutting furniture in half, with the sound volume increasing dramatically. As Haneke says to Toubiana, "Whatever story you tell, there's already been one like it. So how do you have a deeper impact on the viewer? One of the possibilities is the rhythm, which is what film is actually all about. It's much closer to music than to literature."

Late in the saga of destruction, several employees from the telephone company come to check on the status of the family's telephone, which, according to Austrian law, must be either operational or immediately removed. Now that we have been absorbed totally by the isolated and warped consciousness of the family—as we saw earlier, Haneke makes it clear that he regards all of this destruction as sad and tragic, hardly a healthy response to the alienation of contemporary life—it's completely logical and emotionally appropriate that we see these men only as blurry outlines through the translucent glass of the front door. To see them in any other manner would reinsert the recognizably human into a scene that has become utterly inhuman.

The family sits in a dark room watching pop singers on the television as Anna gives Evi a little drink, presumably to put her to sleep so that she won't feel the poison-filled syringe going into her arm. The juxtaposition of this immensely tragic situation and the frivolous program on television is powerful. Evi says her night prayer one last time. We watch Meatloaf singing on the television, while the still hand of Evi and the nearby syringe wordlessly indicate that she is dead.

At this point, the camera cuts once more to the "Australia" image, with the sea moving, but this time it produces no sound of the waves. Anna struggles to take the overdose of pills, and in an extraordinary and upsetting acting tour-de-force she manages to choke them all down, before beginning to keen over her dead daughter. Next we see Georg, leaning up against the wall as though half-dead, as we listen to Anna's death rattle. In one of the most powerful images in the film, we see him scrawling "Anna 12.1.89 2h" (meaning that she has died at 2:00 A.M. on January 12, 1989), while just above, we see that he has already written "Evi 11.1.89 22h" (10:00 P.M. on January 11). He finally adds "Georg?" as the screen once again goes to black.

As Georg lays dying in front of another screen, the television screen filled with visual static, he has a series of flashbacks on earlier, usually more neutral visual images in the film (perhaps an aesthetic error on Haneke's part at this emotional juncture?), which primarily seem to focus on Evi, as well as the now iconic image of "Australia." The final thing we see is a close-up on the television static. The technical *means* of communication is present, perhaps ubiquitous, but no communication is taking place (and wouldn't be, even if something were visible on the screen). Along with the incessant news presented on the radio throughout the film, ending on this image is a strong inkling of the media critique that will become a staple of many of Haneke's subsequent films.

The screen goes black for the last time, and we read this crawl: "The S. family was found on February 17, 1989. Because of the wife's brother's concerns, the house was broken into. The family was buried on February 20. Georg S.'s parents, despite the farewell letter he left behind, did not believe that it was suicide, and filed a murder complaint against 'unknown persons' with the police. The investigation which the police undertook because of this complaint yielded no results. The case was placed in the Unresolved Files section."

In this efficient way, Haneke seems to call upon the dry and supremely scant legal facts to countersign for the essential veracity of the event we have just witnessed, if not for the exactitude of the imagined details. He is telling us, once again, that nothing can ever be fully explained or understood.

Benny's Video (1992)

In vivid contrast to the bright colors and cool compositions of *The Seventh Continent*, *Benny's Video*, Haneke's second feature film, begins with a jerky, grainy, out-of-focus "home video" of a hog being dragged into a killing pen and shot through the head with a bolt from a gun designed especially for slaughtering animals. As with many of the films made by Haneke's aesthetic mentor Antonioni, it's as though this opening sequence were intended to serve as an interpretive key, teaching us how to watch what will follow. Not surprisingly, it is a powerful, even shocking scene—especially since we have no context for discerning who shot the footage, for whom, and who is watching. It doesn't lose its intensity after many viewings, or after all these questions have been answered.

Nor does the video ever seem to lose its interest for Benny (Arno Frisch), the teenaged boy, presumably from Vienna, who seems to have shot the footage and around whose troubled life Haneke's film revolves. An unseen dog barks furiously, and disturbingly, on the sound track of the video, demonstrating once again that Haneke's most chilling effects are achieved through aural means at least as often as through visual ones—and that violence can be heard as well as seen. Shot in the head, the pig falls suddenly in a heap. At this point, rapid rewind, indicated by lines in the image, is employed by unknown hands (a gesture that looks forward to *Caché*), and the shot is replayed in slow motion, with the attendant otherworldly elongation of the sound effects, which lend a solemnity, or perhaps a pregnant enormity, to the proceedings.

Artificially slowed down, the shot that kills the animal now sounds like an elongated clap of rolling thunder, while intermittent snowflakes add a bizarre touch. As Haneke tells Serge Toubiana in the interview that accompanies the Kino DVD of the film, the scene with the pig essentially becomes "playable." "It's a good image for the whole system of the film," he continues, "to make reality into something 'playable.' The danger, of course, is to approach reality that way." At this point, visual static suddenly takes over the screen—Haneke's universal signifier for the medium as such, as pure form—and in bright red letters we read "BENNY'S VIDEO," followed by an identification of Haneke as screenwriter and director—the complete artist, in other words, behind this work of art.

Throughout the film, the image often changes, without warning, from an obviously professional one shot by a thirty-five-millimeter studio camera to amateurish video footage. One effect of this visual instability is to make us rethink the relation of "reality" to the image-making device, especially since the home video (usually assumed to be somehow closer to reality) is itself always embedded within the larger, more-encompassing professional framework of the Haneke film called *Benny's Video.* In other words, we always see Benny's homemade video footage via Haneke's thirty-five-millimeter film, and therefore in its context. Any fixed notion of what constitutes realism immediately goes out the window amid these self-reflexive balls within hollow balls, an image that is made materially explicit when we see balls of this sort taken from the purse of the unnamed girl Benny murders. This destabilization of the image and its source will become a major motif in several of Haneke's films.

We next watch video of Benny's sister (whose identity and relation to Benny we only discover later—a favorite Hanekean delaying device) as she tries to sell her friends, at a party, on the idea of "the pilot's game," which appears to be some sort of Ponzi or pyramid scheme. A regular "studio" shot reveals that we are watching this footage on a television in Benny's well-appointed room, and his mother (Angela Winkler) asks him to switch back to commercial television. There we watch a news announcer reporting a story about football hooligans beating up asylum seekers. Dad (Ulrich Mühe) enters, and what ensues seems at first like the noncommunication typical between teenagers and their parents. However, as they watch, mesmerized by the medium, and the father asks if anything has happened, the mother responds in a monotone voice, "I don't know. Nothing." As such, her response seems meant as part of a developing Haneke critique of the empty form of television news that endlessly repeats itself with apparently different content each time, but whose fixed formal structure prevents any real difference—and thus, real communication—from appearing.

We next see Benny among his classmates in a locker room and at a McDonald's restaurant, which, when the film was made, would have registered as a more powerful critique of American global commercial imperialism than it does now, when most contemporary European teenagers reportedly don't even realize that McDonald's is an American corporation, regarding it simply as a neutral part of the indigenous local commercial landscape they've always known. As in *The Seventh Continent*, an extreme close-up focuses on the cash register, the amount, and then, shot from above, the brightly colored "Guten Appetit" of the paper tray liner, which is presumably intended to international-ize the various standardized (American) products. However, this par-ticular similarity—the intense focus on objects—to Haneke's previous film makes us realize, precisely because it is so infrequent in *Benny's Video*, that the director's interests and critique have shifted firmly in the direction of images—toward *representation*, in other words, rather than remaining with the three-dimensional manufactured objects, so ubiquitous in *The Seventh Continent*.

Next we cut suddenly—once again, without any framing context—to a violent video of a car chase in a B-grade American action movie from the 1970s. This seems to be Haneke's standard pattern: the image first exists on its own, and we gather what meaning and associations, on an immediate, presumably more visceral level—and yet more abstract, because unidentified, level as well—that we can from it. It is only after-ward that we discover that Benny is in a video store sampling the wares, knowledge that contextualizes the clip narratively in terms of the outer film called *Benny's Video*, giving it a more particularized meaning in terms of Benny's character, his individual psychology, and the story he's involved in. Haneke produces his usual overhead, impersonal close-ups on the financial transaction, and it is here that Benny first spots the unnamed girl (Ingrid Stassner)—whom he will later invite to his family's apartment for an innocent encounter that turns deadly—as she intently watches an unseen video from outside the store.

The apartment that Benny and his well-to-do family occupy is filled with the kind of bright breakfast service that we saw in *The Seventh Continent*. The kitchen is ultramodern, silvery, metallic, and shiny, as are the main glass doors, leading to the street, through which these affluent people come and go. The dining room is filled with images, largely taken from Old Master prints, which Benny often glances at, briefly but perhaps pointedly, throughout the film. This could be an unsophisticated attempt by Haneke to produce a (perhaps rather facile) comparison between older, more organic images from high art and newer, vacuous commercial images, but it may also be a comment on the ways in which these venerable artistic images, presumably originally produced for more purely aesthetic reasons, have also been commercialized.

Related to this critique of present-day society in light of the past is the classical choral music we hear while Benny traverses the noisy city streets—a glorious Baroque piece that produces a contrapuntal clash between visuals and aural track, which turns out to be an unusually long sound bridge to the next scene, of a chorale group rehearsing in Benny's school. Extending the critical juxtaposition, Haneke cuts constantly from the cherubic faces singing this aesthetically powerful music to the anonymous exchange of money among the older choristers that seems to be part of the never-explained "pilot game" that is a running but incomprehensible motif throughout.

What follows is the central scene of the film. It begins with Benny inviting the girl up to his family's apartment. Interestingly, we first see them talking through the video store's front window, but we can't hear what Benny is saying—it's as though Haneke knows that the content of the exchange can be nothing more than banal, with no real communicative content, and wants, as he often says, for us to use our imagination instead. Once in the apartment, she is entranced by all the "cool" video equipment that Benny's wealthy parents have bought for him, and when she explains that her commute into the city is at least an hour each way, via several different means of transportation, we feel Haneke nodding gently but not really too seriously in the direction of a more traditional leftist critique of class relations. In any case, her plight seems to hold little interest for Benny, and the subject is changed.

She is especially impressed by the camera that Benny has trained on the street below, which shows simply what is happening in real time. Haneke tells Toubiana that "Benny thinks he can control things by incorporating them into video, for example, with the camera on the street. Of course, it's an illusion, even a dangerous illusion. Why do people film their vacations? I've never done that, nor even taken pictures. I find that totally perverse. [I think the idea they have is that] if I have an image of that, I possess it. Naturally, that's ridiculous. It's a very strong desire, caused, I think, by the media. We see the world via the media, so we're in danger of thinking that only through the media is there a reality. But it's exactly the opposite."

Benny shows off in front of his new friend with traditional, mildly rebellious adolescent behavior such as smoking, and Haneke seems to

Figure 3. The Girl (Ingrid Stassner) enters Benny's (Arno Frisch) world of video in *Benny's Video*.

be establishing a kind of line between "normal" teenage nonconformity and the much sicker variety that Benny will soon rather haphazardly undertake. She decides to stay "just because," as she vaguely puts it, and they eat pizza (an operation to which Haneke devotes close attention, as he does to the transactions in stores, as though these mundane gestures might somehow become revelatory), and then Benny begins to act out a series of jokes about people on the subway. Suddenly, he violently grabs her, ostensibly miming the vignette that he calls "cop on the U-Bahn," but the suddenness of the aggressive gesture, which will become an important Haneke signature in some of the later films, constitutes a minor but unnerving surprise to the viewer and hints of worse to come.

This uncomfortably personal, one-on-one encounter seems painfully awkward to both parties, even beyond the obvious explanation of their youth. One of the things being demonstrated here is that we do act differently before others than we do before a recorded image. As Haneke explains to Toubiana: "We allow ourselves feelings when facing an image, but not a person, because it's more dangerous, since the image can no longer react. The image is finished, so you can be relaxed. In principle, that's where all horror films come from, because you can take pleasure in the horror because you can be sure that it can't do anything to you. . . . But if we try to do that with the things in our life, obviously it's extremely dangerous. And that's sort of the story that's told in *Benny's Video*."

The teenagers examine the video of the slaughtered hog, once again "playing" with the represented reality—making it "playable," in Haneke's phrase—as at the beginning of the film, by rewinding, running it in slow motion, distorting the sound, and so on. It's so similar to the opening sequence that the earlier clip may even have been, we suddenly realize, a flash-forward to what we're seeing now.

When the girl asks Benny "what it was like with the pig," a question that Haneke believes is central to the meaning of the film when applied to the death of the girl, Benny just shrugs and says, "It was only a pig." The relation of reality and its media representation is further thematized when Benny strangely begins talking about the tricks of plastic and ketchup that are used in action films to represent violence. Each of them admits that neither has seen death "in reality," and Benny recounts the story of being hoisted up by his father to see his dead grandfather in his casket. "Ich habe die Augen zugemacht," Benny says; "I closed my eyes." The reality of death is obviously more difficult to deal with than its cinematic representation.

At this point, Benny offers to show her something, the fetishized "thing" he has stolen, the special gun used to slaughter the pig. He gives it to her to shoot him (we see all this in "reality," that is, in Haneke's film through his thirty-five-millimeter camera, *and* on the monitor behind them), and when she doesn't, he playfully calls her a coward. She hands it back to him, then says, "You press it," and calls him "coward," again playfully, in turn. At that point, he nonchalantly points and fires the gun,winces at the report, and the girl falls with the sudden heaviness of the pig.

Haneke's camera shows us this scene on the monitor as well, then slowly pans left so that we see most of everything that follows on the video monitor alone, as though the mediatized representation has replaced the too-difficult "reality." Of course, this reality would in any case come to us via Haneke's film called *Benny's Video*, and thus would remain always a mediatized representation. Nevertheless, *within the frame of the fiction* of Haneke's film, we too have now become implicated in the substitution of the representation of violence for the "real" violence, especially if we find ourselves wanting to see the "real thing" yet having to content ourselves with its video representation on Benny's monitor. The girl struggles, and at first he tries to help her as she screams like a wounded animal—in a manner guaranteed to upset any audience—and the entire scene then moves off the monitor as well. Suddenly we are reduced to "reading" the sound alone, yet the power of the scene seems enhanced rather than diminished.

Yelling "quiet!" we hear him begin to hit her, and we see him run across the monitor screen to reload the gun. Another blast, more screaming, and more shouts of "quiet!" (He also says "bitte, bitte"—please, please—which would seem to indicate that he is panicking and thus not totally culpable of cold-blooded murder.) He runs across the monitor and reloads yet again, with the girl's sobs and cries continuing, until a third loud bang suddenly stops all noise, and we know, through the sound alone (or, rather, its complete absence) that she is dead. The camera remains on the empty monitor for a while as we hear the gun dropping, and then finally, on the lower left-hand corner of the monitor, we see Benny leaning, exhausted, against the wall.

Haneke explains the complexity of this scene in some detail to Toubiana. "Of course, the idea is to make the viewer aware that he's watching an artifact and not reality, because it's a double screen—he's watching the screen, and in the image, there's another screen. That's a way of making the viewer aware of where he is, especially in the scenes where there's the danger that he will be totally manipulated by the feelings that are aroused. There we're practically obligated to make him aware of his role." An important topos for Haneke is sounded here for the first time: the ethics of filmmaking, certainly ("we're practically obligated"), but also the interconnectedness of artistic manipulation and viewer responsibility, conveyed through an almost Brechtian *Verfremdungs-Effekt* ("alienation effect" is the usual, though misleading, translation) that occurs via the doubling of the visual image.

The sound track is at least as crucial to this whole process as the visual track, and they work in perfect counterpoint. "In this case," Haneke continues, "it's the image that is distancing, and it is the sound that is the manipulation. And with these two means, it gives an impression that's complex enough to destabilize the viewer. With the image, you cut the imagination short. With the image, you see what you see, and it's 'reality.' With sound, as with words, you incite the imagination. That's why it's more useful for me, if I want to touch someone emotionally, to use sound rather than image. We always know the image is manipulated, and [Benny] even speaks of it in the film: he says, 'I saw something about cinema,' and 'it's all ketchup,' et cetera."

But a question arises. As long as the sound has such a powerful, manipulative effect on us, as the director puts it, is it still possible to maintain that the violence in Haneke's films is always "offscreen" and therefore "nonexploitative"? A definitive answer to this question is impossible, but it's clear that sound constitutes much more than an "incitement to the imagination," for it too is a representation—in fact, it is a kind of "immediate" representation (in semiotic terms, an indexical rather than a conventional sign—and an extremely powerful one) that doesn't rely on codes or signs as much as visual images do.

What follows in the film is a series of gestures that indicate either

Benny's lack of concern or his state of shock—depending, Haneke would undoubtedly say, on how an individual viewer wants to interpret it. He drinks some water, in a deliberate fashion, and slowly eats his yogurt. He brutally goes through the girl's belongings, one of the gestures that, for this viewer at least, most powerfully signals his culpability—but other gestures lead toward an opposite conclusion. He does his homework, to the sounds of heavy metal rock music, and then nonchalantly spends some time cleaning up the girl's blood. Haneke extracts the maximum horror from this action by showing her body being violently pulled across the floor trailing a smear of blood, but without showing anyone actually pulling her; the bloody image, emptied of a visual causal explanation for her movement, seems even more disturbing. Presumably we are being made to use our imagination once again, because we can't fully see what's happening.

So is Benny truly culpable, or was it merely an accident, and he simply panicked? In short, why did he do it? Haneke explains to Toubiana, "I always want to leave open the answer to the question, 'Why did someone do something?' In this case, [any] answer is only there to reassure and to calm the viewer. To say, 'His mommy didn't love her little boy enough,' is ridiculous. That's not it. I think the reason for a crime or an accident is always much more complex than what you can describe in seventy minutes."

In an apparent desire for some form of spiritual or perhaps merely physical purgation, Benny takes off every bit of his clothing and continues to clean up the girl's blood. The camera cuts, without narrative motivation, to the high-art images along the dining room wall and then, possibly implying a link, back to Benny, who discovers a smear of blood on his naked side, in the exact spot that traditional Christian iconography shows the spear wound on Christ's crucified body. A close-up of a video image of him wiping the blood from his side follows, and he also modestly pulls down the dead girl's skirt before turning her over to videotape her, still covered in blood: a delicate gesture, in short, followed by another horrifying one. The image is suddenly rewound at high speed, as he did with the video of the pig, and we realize that the time period has shifted, and Benny is studying the images later, as though he were editing a film or video, making reality "playable"—and keeping us guessing—in the same manner as Haneke's later film, *Caché*.

At some point after the girl's death, Benny pours himself a glass of milk, and the frame is saturated with blue and white hues. When he wipes up some spilled milk, the gesture reminds us of the blood he has just wiped up. This barrage of various hues makes us aware of a kind of muted symphony of color that Haneke constructs in the film, composed especially in blue and black.

After Toubiana comments that "there's no warmth at all in the image. It's important for it to be icy," Haneke replies, "The whole trilogy is like that. It's a little colder than reality. That's because, especially on TV, everything is a little warmer than in reality, so it was an artificial means by which to create more distance and also more clarity. Because if an image is bluer, it seems sharper. If it's more red or yellow, it seems more blurred, more pleasant. And the 'surgical' view that some have reproached me for may come partly from this. The frames always seem very sharp, as though you're looking at them from a distance. By contrast, the videos in *Benny's Video* aren't as cold as that."

After a quick trip to a rock club with his friend Ricci, followed by a sleepover at Ricci's parents' apartment, he goes to visit his sister. He seems to want to discuss what has happened, but for various reasons he is unable to. His next striking if ambiguous gesture is to have his head shaved in a barber shop located in the subway, which results in an image with contradictory interpretive possibilities. He seems to have become both skinhead and Auschwitz victim.

His father is not pleased with what he calls Benny's new "concentration camp" look (yet, abetting the ambiguity, he also castigates him for "protesting"), and, as Haneke's example of the ultra-bourgeois so typically despised by most Austrian writers and artists, he tells Benny, "Seriously, don't give me that teenage stuff about not being loved. People have to agree on certain things. Provided one is reasonably intelligent, which you won't deny you are, one sticks to the rules, if one wants others to stick to them too, particularly when it takes so little effort."

After talking with (or rather listening to) his father, Benny finally asks, "Can I go now?"—the same bored-teenager question he will ask at the police station at the end of the film, after he has betrayed his parents. For Haneke, the head-shaving gesture is purposely ambiguous and intended to foreground the role of the audience in constructing meaning: "You can interpret that in several ways: as self-punishment to make himself like a prisoner, it's a sort of public self-declaration of guilt. You can also see it as a protest. The viewer has to decide. I'm always looking for a way to tell the story where I put the questions back to the viewer. I don't want to tell him, 'Now you must think this. Now the boy thinks that.' It's up to the viewer to decide" (Toubiana interview). Some viewers, of course, may, legitimately or not, be dismayed by Haneke's constant, principled abdication of the artist's traditional responsibility to create (specific) meaning(s).

More images—a Donald Duck comic book in German and some television news clips about Serbian troops—lead to another crucial moment in the film, when Benny's parents find him watching his video of the girl's death and demand to see it for themselves. While replaying it, Benny's eyes blink, as before, when the first shot is fired. Haneke's camera alternates among Benny's downcast looks, the monitor, and his parents watching raptly (but always separately, never in a two-shot), simultaneously horrified and entranced. When the tape ends and Haneke has the monitor switch automatically and jarringly back to regular TV and its usual vapid images, he seems to be proposing a purposely obscene equivalence between the killing of the girl and a newscast. In so doing, he once again criticizes a media form that transforms all reality before it into its mere representation, where all images have equal force, value, and truth. In this fashion, Haneke might say, all reality can be transmuted into its harmless, apparently equivalent simulacrum that we can easily control because it is already fixed in place, at least in our present-day mediatized society. Even if the specific content seems to change, in other words, media form is itself so powerful that all differences in content are ultimately canceled out, and any truth disappears.

Haneke spells out his larger intentions to Christopher Sharrett in a remarkably direct fashion:

> I am most concerned with television as the key symbol primarily of the media representation of violence [especially in *Benny's Video* and *Funny Games*], and more generally of a greater crisis, which I see as our collective loss of reality and social disorientation. Alienation is a very complex problem, but television is certainly implicated in it.
>
> We don't, of course, anymore perceive reality, but instead the rep-

resentation of reality in television. Our experiential horizon is very limited. What we know of the world is little more than the mediated world, the image. We have no reality, but a derivative of reality, which is extremely dangerous, most certainly from a political standpoint but in a larger sense to our ability to have a palpable sense of the truth of everyday experience.

Haneke's argument is compelling, but it also seems to rely upon the notion that reality, even the everyday variety, is or was ever available to us or our forebears in some kind of direct and unmediated form. In this respect, Haneke's views smack of the theories of Guy DeBord, in *The Society of the Spectacle*, and Jean Baudrillard more generally, both of whom attack the "simulacrum" of reality that has supposedly displaced our putative, prior direct apprehension of reality.

However, many other theorists, like Jacques Derrida, to cite one example, seriously doubt that such direct access to reality is or has ever been available. Technology of some sort, no matter how primitive, must always intervene, and any reality must also always be framed to be perceived. Haneke's apparent naiveté in longing for a lost, golden, *im*-mediate world—a longing that remains common—is seen even more clearly in one of the interviews translated for this volume: "I belong to a generation that was able to grow up without the continuous presence of television. I was thus able to apprehend the world directly, without an intermediary. Today, on the other hand, children learn to know reality through films, and reality is presented on television in two different ways: there is the reality of documentary shows and the reality of fictional images. I think that the media has played an important role in this loss of a sense of reality."

But what about films that were made before television's arrival? What about radio, and the "you-are-there," supposedly direct presentations of reality in the reports by Edward R. Murrow during the Battle of Britain? We have always processed (and *must* always process) raw reality, or what the French psychoanalyst Jacques Lacan would call the Real, through a host of filtering devices (including language, ideology, religion, ideas about visual perspective developed during the Renaissance, and so on), and contemporary media are only more sophisticated, more technologically advanced versions of these "filters," without which we would be unable to see anything.

Moving back to the specific events of *Benny's Video*, Haneke tells Toubiana that Benny's decision to show the film to his parents has, once again, several possible motivations. "On the one hand, perhaps it's out of fear, an inability to speak about it, but at the same time it's a gigantic provocation. . . . How do you react if your child shows you this act? That makes it more real [to the audience] than when [we] saw the act itself. . . . You're shocked the first time, but I was much more upset the second time, when the parents watch it."

At this point, the father takes over and attempts to buck up the failing spirits of his tremulous wife. Like any good, optimistic bourgeois, he is filled with a kind of can-do, ultra-rational spirit, which—though he claims several times that he too is doubtful about what course they should take—never considers ethical or moral issues and sees everything in practical, purely technical terms. In this way, it's similar to the Pentagon Papers that were leaked to the *New York Times* during the Vietnam War. As with these papers that considered strategies for conducting the war, Benny's father's only thought is, "How can we most expeditiously deal with this situation that confronts us?" It's clear that Haneke is also offering a disguised but real critique of the kind of technocratic thinking that could eventuate in the unthinkable—the Holocaust, and, in more specific terms, Austria's ongoing refusal to confront its part in that immense tragedy.

Haneke tells Toubiana that when the film premiered in Vienna, people asked only mundane technical questions. "At one point, I said, 'Don't you want to talk about this Austrian habit of sweeping unpleasant things under the carpet?' Total silence. After a very long pause, they started to ask me nonsense questions again. Everywhere else, the first question wasn't about the video and all that, it was about Austria's past. That was strange, and it surprised me a great deal. Or, rather, it confirmed for me that I was right to talk about it."

The parents' discussion about the proper course of action is shot in separate close-ups, never in a two-shot. The father says, "Do you realize he'll be ruined for life? Not to mention all the other consequences." "It would do wonders for our reputations!" he adds sarcastically (in the German dialogue, significantly, the word translated as "reputations" in the subtitles also means "image"). Though more emotionally upset, the wife also considers only the practical aspects of the matter and wonders how her husband will get the body out of the apartment. We could burn her things, he says, and his wife helpfully, ghoulishly, brings up the question of dismemberment and how the bones might be dealt with. They do realize at some level the gravity of what they are discussing (if not their own moral responsibility), and she asks her husband whether he is really serious about all this. He replies that he doesn't know and asks, "Do you have another alternative?" She shrugs her shoulders and suggests that they get some sleep. The husband asks again, "Can you cope? Will you be able to stomach it? The pieces will have to be very small, and I have no idea how long it will take."

It is apparently decided that Mom and Benny will head off to a holiday in Egypt while Dad stays home and does the dirty work. Before they depart, Dad confronts Benny about having tried to see his sister Evi, which could have compromised their situation. Violently grabbing Benny's face, he shouts, "You must not lie!" because Benny has said nothing about the attempted visit. Haneke's irony is at its peak during this display of middle-class hypocrisy.

When Benny and his mother get to Egypt, almost everything we see is from inside the tour bus, Haneke's camera shooting through the window past Benny, onto the "reality" that is being commercially transformed into a packaged "experience" for tourists. The exotic other becomes processed image, safely on the other side of the "screen" constituted by the window. As an image it comes prepackaged and, like genre movies, is expected to follow certain clear rules (like staying on the other side of the window).

Benny continues his own videotaping of the various people and things he encounters in Egypt, including a man flying in a large kite pulled by a boat, the market and its exotic denizens, and several mosques, all to the accompaniment of strange classical organ music on the sound track. His mother tapes the inhabitants of a primitive village, and the sound of a dog barking offscreen recalls to us the disturbing braying of the dog in the video of the hog's slaughter. (Again, Haneke achieves an important effect through aleatory sound.) They play backgammon, swim, and Benny at one point even attempts to videotape his mother while she's urinating. He manages to send a desultory video greeting back to his father. Interestingly, the contrast ratio is so extreme that the image is barely visible; in fact, it's not completely clear that this video is really addressed to his father at all.

All of this organized recreation, we soon realize, is meant to block out the reality that is presumably going on back home as Dad, piece by piece, gets rid of the girl's body. At one point, Haneke's camera holds on mother and son lying on adjoining single beds, side by side, as they watch Egyptian television for what seems like a very long time. Imperceptibly—this is the dramatic purpose of the brilliant extended long-take—the mother begins to break down emotionally and ends up sobbing violently. Benny wants to do something to help her, and even reaches out to try to touch her. He seems upset over the intensity of her emotional response. This is perhaps the moment of his own *prise de conscience*, his first full realization of the enormity of what has happened, and thus the point that leads him finally to decide to denounce his parents to the police, which he does at the end of the film. (As usual, though, this can only be surmised, and there is no overt textual information to support such a reading.)

Haneke tells Toubiana that "in principle, that's the theme of all my films: guilt. How do you deal with this, your own sense of becoming guilty, no matter what the topic? I come from a Judeo-Christian culture, so it's normal to speak of that. And the passage in Egypt is a kind of sign of that: he runs away to avoid responsibility, but he becomes guiltier by doing it. The mother knows what the father is going to do. [Benny] knows more than his parents what it's all about, what his father is doing. But at the same time, he wants to deny his own guilt, because he says, 'I didn't want to. It was a moment.' The scene of the murder is filmed in such a way that it's left open. Even he seems to be surprised. Did he really want to do that? I always try [to show that] the act that makes us feel guilty is ambiguous."

When they arrive home, Benny opens the door and seems over-whelmed by the artificial light and the harshly reflective surfaces all around him. Is this a response to his recent sojourn in the desert, where all was different, perhaps more organic and premodern? Mom is chipper again, though Dad seems extremely grave. "I'm glad you're home," he says. "Me, too," Benny responds noncommittally. Dad then says, "Good, I love you," but he gets no response. "Sleep well, then, everything's okay. You don't have anything to worry about." What comes next, according to Haneke, is one of the most important exchanges in the film. Father: "I wanted to ask you something. Why did you do it?" Benny: "What? I don't know. I wanted probably to see what it is like." Father: "How what is?" Benny shrugs.

Haneke tells Toubiana that something similar he read in the newspaper originally led him to make the film. "I started collecting stories like this, and the sentence kept reappearing: 'I wanted to know what it was like.' Only someone who is out of contact with reality could say that. One only learns about life and reality [nowadays] by means of the media, and you have the sense that you are missing something, that you lack the feeling of reality. When you see only images, even a documentary, you're always outside. And [these people were saying] I wanted at least one time to find out what it was like to be inside. That's what got me interested in making the film."

The obvious question, though, is why this desire to know, for example, what murdering someone is like was never much in evidence before the advent of modern media. Is it perhaps not so much that the media has substituted itself for reality but that it represents violent, *nonordinary* reality in such a tantalizing way that makes people want to experience it? This is not at all the same thing.

Life seems to quickly get back to normal for Benny, and we soon see him with his friend Ricci, listening to heavy metal in his room (now the doors partially block our view) and watching videos of his sister's pilot game with which the film began. Shots of what seems to be a rather stupid party are overlaid with the baroque choral music we heard earlier (making the contrast between the two eras deeply and perhaps a bit too earnestly ironic), with the choral music serving once again as an extended sound bridge. We cut to individual shots of children's singing faces, bathed in light, as Benny's family listens to the concert.

We then cut to a video of the corner of Benny's bed, and we are surprised to discover that he had earlier recorded his mother's and his father's voices, from his room, as they plotted what to do with the girl's body. Suddenly the voices get louder and somewhat different in sound quality, while we still see the same unchanging video image. We realize that this new video is being played for the benefit of the police, whose questions, very similar to the earlier grilling Benny had undergone at the hands of his father, now take over the sound track. "Why did you come to us?" they demand, and he replies with the same noncommittal phrase used by the murdered girl, explaining why she has decided to stay in Benny's apartment: "Just because." After he tells them where his parents can be found, he asks, "Can I go now?"

In his interview with Toubiana, Haneke refuses to spell out the meaning of Benny's gesture. "Is he naive? Is it cynicism? You can take it as you like." And beyond this particular scene, there is also a practical reason, according to the director, why he refuses to explain. Toubiana theorizes that "in place of psychology in your films, people *do* things. And that takes the place of an explanation." Haneke responds, "Yes, because film is visual. Explanation is all right with words in a book, where you can explain a lot. In film you have to show things."

We next cut to video shots of the trip to Egypt; perhaps Haneke wants to underline, once again, as with the city streets and the baroque music, the obvious contrasts between the world of the past and the world of the present, between the third world that Benny and his mother have glimpsed and the advanced, inauthentic industrial society in which they live. We see mother, father, and son in individual close-ups outside the police office, and Benny says merely "Entschuldigung" to

Figure 4. Benny (Arno Frisch)
in his element in *Benny's Video*.

his parents on his way out, which is the kind of banal phrase ("excuse me") used in German when someone is accidentally bumped, but hardly an expression of real sorrow.

The film closes with a long-take of a central monitor, which shows the parents, in a high-angle shot, as they are led into a room for questioning, with parts of two other monitors visible on either side and the radio news telling us more about the war in Bosnia and about some people who have been killed in a tram disaster in Sweden. Reality, even as we watch, is being turned into spectacle and representation and thus made unreal. Suddenly, the words "BENNY'S VIDEO" appear in bright red letters on the central monitor, just as they did at the start of the film. The credits roll, and the film, rather than sharply concluding, gradually peters out—significantly, on the monitors—once there is nothing left to see.

71 *Fragments of a Chronology of Chance* (1994)

For the third film in what Haneke has called a trilogy that represents "my portrait of the society in which I live" and whose topic is "communication which doesn't communicate" (Toubiana interview on *71 Fragments* DVD), the director expands his lens beyond the narrow, even obsessive focus on individual, if typical, families that occupied the first two films to take up "a cross-section of society." The film is about "coldness," according to the director, and this noncommunicating communication "is my strongest feeling, and I always try to deal with it in my films. We talk and talk, but we don't communicate. And the closer you get, the worse it is." This non- or countercommunication, in other words, goes beyond the media to infect individuals and society as a whole.

Like *The Seventh Continent* and, in a more general sense, *Benny's Video*, *71 Fragments* is based on a real event, an "inexplicable" murderous rampage in a bank by a Viennese military cadet on December 23, 1993. Looked at from a typical Haneke viewpoint, the film is a kind of amorphous, fragmentary, and highly abstract "nonexplanation" of the tragedy. Haneke has the usual suspects in mind—the media above all— but as is his wont, he seeks (though he doesn't always succeed) to present viewers with the maximum ambiguity so that they will be required to construct and make sense of the fragments of understanding on their own, rather than have it done for them. Unlike *The Seventh Continent*, the factual information underlying this story is presented in an intertitle *before* the film proper begins. The opening, sober black-and-white title reads: "On 12–23–93, Maximilian B., a 19-year-old student, shot three people in a Viennese bank and killed himself with a shot in the head shortly afterward."

This intertitle seems to perform two related functions. First, it guarantees the non-frivolousness of what we are about to see. The events with which the film culminates actually took place, Haneke insists more clearly than ever, and this connection to "reality" profoundly orients our way of watching the film and the terms upon which we accept or reject it. Second, *71 Fragments* is by far Haneke's most overtly "experimental" and least explicitly narrative film, at least among those made for theatrical release, in that it does indeed consist of exactly seventy-one fragments, some long, some ultrashort, and some medium length, whose relevance or "glue" is only barely recognizable in the context of the factual information with which the film begins, and only with considerable effort on the part of the viewer as it proceeds.

One element emphasized in the film's title is *chronology*, which provides another organizing device—besides the gradual coming together of an inchoate, virtual narrative sense—that structures the film. The seventy-one fragments are thus divided into five different days, all from 1993: October 12, October 26, October 30, November 17, and, finally, December 23, the day on which the "inexplicable" slaughter occurs. One of the few quasi-reliable ways of looking at and organizing reality, or at least its temporal or durational aspect, Haneke seems to be saying, is through the fixity of dates, even if this forward-marching, apparently logical organization of life ultimately leads to little more than utter *chance*, that other foregrounded word that sits at the title's end.

In this contradictory, fragmentarily experienced and ultimately unknowable world, nothing does finally add up, hence whatever does happen can only be a result of chance. (A Hollywood film like *Signs* [dir. M. Night Shyamalan, 2002] takes the opposite position: while all *seems* inexplicable and random, actually everything has a hidden purpose, and if we only properly read the "signs" that have been lavished upon us by a deity or other unknown entity, we can understand everything.) For Haneke, as for many modernists, our sole recourse against the debilitating randomness of the universe is the self-conscious *chosenness* and deliberateness of art, so much on display in *71 Fragments*. Thus, one specific force structurally working against, or in constant tension with, the idea of chance in this film is the number, length, and placement of Haneke's carefully chosen fragments, all neatly arranged in chronological order.

The title of the film and the opening credits do not appear until fragment 4, as we follow an unknown truck through the familiar Hanekean blue-black night into an unknown city. The truck contains a young boy; we later find out he is a Romanian national who has illegally crossed the border into Austria. Many fragments after that, we learn that his name is Marian Radu. (We have also seen him crossing a river at night in fragment 2, which contains three shots, and ensconcing himself in the truck, which is delivering washing machines to Vienna, in fragment 3, comprised of only one shot.)

All of the important "characters"—important only because they end up, by chance, being at the bank on the fateful day of the student's killing spree, or are connected to someone who is—thus begin to appear, one by one. Throughout the film, little of this—for example, who the main

Figure 5. The Romanian boy (Gabriel Cosmin Urdes) adrift in Vienna in *71 Fragments of a Chronology of Chance*.

characters are—is signaled in any direct fashion. In fact, much of what we can be said to know about this story comes only in retrospect, after the film has concluded. If occasionally annoying, this is very much part of Haneke's theme of the final and irrevocable unknowability of events and other human beings, including the reasons behind the "inexplicable" slaughter at the bank, as the television news will describe it at the end of the film.

Besides the Romanian boy and the young military cadet who turns killer, Maximilian B., the fragments follow a kind, deeply feeling woman and her husband, who are moved by the Romanian boy's plight, which they've witnessed on television, to become temporary foster parents for him. Another person whom we follow is a middle-aged bank guard, Hans Nohal (a name we learn only from an ID card flashed near the end of the film), who is married and has a baby.

We also, in a manner of speaking, follow the story—a "story," like the others, which consists of little more than banal episodes of daily life—of an elderly and disgruntled gentleman who has emotional difficulties with his daughter, who works in the same bank. (When we initially see them interact at her counter in the bank, we have no idea that they are related.) Since, by the end of the film, we know that all three of these people whose mundane lives we trace—the kind woman, the bank guard, and the old man—happen to be in the bank on the day of the killings, and since we know from the opening explanatory titles that Maximilian B. kills three people before killing himself, we *surmise*, since we've been following them, that these are the three who will be killed.

Yet, with the exception of the guard—a small corner of whose lifeless body we see lying on the floor, a body that we are able to identify solely through the color of the uniform, which is now steadily emitting a fatal stream of blood—Haneke gives us no direct evidence that the kind woman and the old man are also killed. He thus continues to demand of his audience, as in his two earlier films, a great deal of epistemological work and cognitive speculation for little immediate payoff. On another level, of course, he offers much more.

Another important theme that can be found in the film's title lies in the word "fragments." Like most poststructuralist theorists, especially perhaps the French literary critic Roland Barthes, Haneke clearly believes that any truth about the world, about reality, is only knowable, if at all, in the form of fragments. His film, like poststructuralist theory, is anti-totalizing in the sense that nothing—no person, no idea, no event—can ever be finally understandable and completely explicable. There is always some important connection missing, some "inconsequential" evidence that it is suppressed because otherwise it would contradict any overarching hypothesis. Haneke is thus saying that, if this is the case for reality itself, then it is a lie to make a film that purports to fully explain anything.

As he tells Toubiana in the interview on the DVD, "We have access to reality only through fragments because it's our day-to-day experience. We see very little; we understand even less. But in mainstream cinema we pretend that we know everything. That bothers me. . . . Only in fragmentation can we tell a story honestly. Showing the little pieces and the sum of these little pieces opens up a little bit the chance for the spectator to choose and to work with his own experiences."

But just as we can only experience "reality" or the "world" or "truth" as a series of fragments, our experience of other people is incomplete and fragmentary as well. Haneke tells Toubiana that we claim that "the character is like *this*. But the character is also like this and this, and all these alsos are often contradictory. That's what makes life so rich and so irritating. It's irritating in a work because we're used to always having the answer as to why a person is like this or that, but we never know why in real life. You can suspect or have an idea, but this idea could be completely wrong."

Another important aspect of the film's ambiguous structure is its division into an unpredictable series of fragments (why seventy-one?) of wildly varying length (some last only a few seconds, while others go on for several minutes), each ending in a cut to black that lasts precisely two seconds (unlike the cuts to black in *The Seventh Continent*, which vary in length). Haneke's recourse for an explanation is to the art of music: "You have a theme and a countertheme, and it's through this structure that you open up the world of the sonata" (DVD interview). One also senses that Haneke has worked out an elaborate musical rhythm tied to the varying length of the fragments, though this would be difficult to chart or verify.

In any case, this conscious structuration or composition can also tell us something about character: "If you show a person in a situation, you don't know about anything except the situation, not the person. For example, this is an interview. But you don't know why the person is there, why he is speaking the way he is, and so on. It's the role of the construction [of the film] to make that contradictory enough to create the illusion of the richness of life" (Toubiana interview).

Yet the director is never interested in structure for its own sake. As always, its functioning must take into account the reactions of the viewer. Haneke may be the contemporary art-film director who is most interested in viewer reaction (in a way that resembles, oddly enough, horror-film directors) and, by extension, exploring the viewer's moral responsibility for his or her reactions and pleasures. "How is the viewer going to react? When you make a film, you always have to keep this in mind. I wanted to create typical and recognizable fragments [that were] not necessarily understandable, but recognizable. That's something else" (DVD interview).

The distinction that Haneke makes here is useful because each fragment is recognizable as an action or gesture in and of itself (a couple is talking in bed; a boy is riding in a car with a woman; a man eats dinner with his wife, then slaps her) but not understandable *overall* in more than a hazy sense until the ending of the film draws them together. This is also the method of the well-known Mexican film *Amores Perros* (dir. Alejandro González Iñárritu, 2000), which followed *71 Fragments* six years later: a series of seemingly unrelated stories (told, however, in a much less fragmented style, and with more clarity and coherence in each individual storyline) only comes together in the final scene, when we understand the nature of the event toward which all their lives have been unconsciously—and randomly—aiming.

Both films, at any rate, as well as Haneke's later film *Code Unknown*, can be contrasted with what have been called "ensemble films," or what Michel Cieutat, in an interview translated in this volume, calls "the choral film." In this interview, Haneke draws a sharp distinction between these two methods: "*71 Fragments* and *Code Unknown* are different from *Short Cuts*, *American Beauty*, or *Magnolia*, a genre that's currently in vogue. These films have a tendency to tie up the strings of all their stories at the end. After finishing *71 Fragments*, I tried to do the opposite, or something much more complicated. I prefer to follow all the strings, in perfect continuity, without losing them, but without ever having to come back to them to tie them up in an explicating way."

In *71 Fragments*, the first overt narrative link between any of the internal stories comes in fragment 34, which opens the third section, October 30, 1993. Here we see a television interview with the Romanian boy, who has turned himself in to the police, and then we cut to the old man (whose daughter works in the bank) watching the interview. This is the first cut within a single fragment to another location, though of course the interview with the Romanian boy could have been showing on the television in the old man's room. Nevertheless, the shift of location—and an extremely tentative hint by Haneke that the media might also possibly help *unite* us and thus be beneficial to society—is confirmed when we cut, still within the same fragment, to a shot of the couple watching the same interview, which leads them to want to do something to help the Romanian boy (unfortunately, this also seems to mean that they reject a young girl they had earlier chosen for adoption).

While most of the fragments emphasize the banality of everyday life, in which "nothing happens," some sequences are striking and even unforgettable. In fragment 19, for example, Haneke employs an extended long-take showing Maximilian B. practicing ping-pong against an automatic machine. Haneke himself has explained (and in the process provided an excellent justification for the sometimes reviled long-take aesthetic) how the viewer goes through several stages watching this ultra-repetitious shot—boredom, anger, laughter—before finally starting to actually *look* at what is going on. "We could have shown the information (that a guy is playing against a machine) in one minute, but because it lasts so long, you understand it differently. The secret is to find the right length in imagining how I as a viewer would react to that. You say okay, then you get bored, then you get angry, you say cut, then after a certain time you start to watch it and feel its pulse. That's the right length, and it's hard to find. . . . That's always the secret, and it's a question of music" (Toubiana interview). Note the ongoing concern with the viewer's reaction. Even more important, the numbing repetition is also clearly meant to emphasize the boredom and repetitiveness of our everyday lives, which is, once again, the method of the film. The most uncanny moments in this fragment come when Maximilian continues to swing like an automaton, even when the machine occasionally fails to deliver a ball.

Two other striking scenes concern the older man and his daughter, Frau Tomek, who works in the bank. In the first one (fragment 12), we can't at first understand why she is using the familiar pronoun "du" with this customer until she later in the fragment addresses him as "father," finally getting rid of him with a promise to call. This sets up fragment 36, in which she does call two weeks later, and which provides perhaps the most overtly emotional moment of the film. Breaking into the middle of this telephone conversation between the old man and his daughter (and occasionally his granddaughter), Haneke never moves the camera for nine long minutes, as the television continues to spew its banalities and the old man whines and wheedles and plays on the daughter's obvious guilt feelings, though we can't make out what she is saying in reply. "I'm sorry for existing," he angrily tells her at one point. The most amazing thing about the fragment is that, according to the director, every word in the father's telephone monologue was scripted in advance, despite its hyper-realistic, improvisational feeling.

One other particularly powerful sequence comes when the bank guard is wordlessly eating dinner with his wife in fragment 38 and is suddenly moved, perhaps owing to the alcohol he has consumed, to whisper "I love you." When she questions him sharply as to why he would say something like that, something he never says, he slaps her in the face. The timing of the two actors is impeccable. Neither says a word after the slap, and eventually she puts her hand on his arm and they quietly resume eating. Maximilian Le Cain has insightfully called the scene "so starkly eloquent in its depiction of true feeling desperately seeking a means of expression that it could stand up as a brilliant short film in its own right." It also provides one of those jump-out-of-your-seat moments that has subsequently become (in *Code Unknown, Caché,* and other films) a signature Haneke gesture.

The cold, mechanistic images of *The Seventh Continent*, which eschew faces to concentrate instead on the sheer facticity of the ubiquitous, bright, and shiny objects in our lives, reappear here in relation to the internal workings of the bank, especially in the emotionless, anonymous exchanges of large sums of money by the bank guard Hans Nohal and others. Nor does Haneke give us much time to identify with the principal characters, just as in *The Seventh Continent*, since, especially in the beginning, we see them only as hands and feet surrounded by domestic appliances, and also because they are rarely onscreen for extended periods of time. (Fragment 7, which shows the bank guard getting dressed in the morning, is almost identical in its anonymity to a sequence from the earlier film.)

Fragment 9 introduces the important motif of the game of correctly putting various pieces (fragments) of a paper cross together—in other words, solving a puzzle, a neat bit of Antonionian instruction in how Haneke expects us to watch the film. It's also a *game*, of course, which will become the overarching motif in Haneke's next film, *Funny Games*. In fragment 23, one of the students again fails to put the fragments of the paper cross together correctly. This sequence is also notable in that it shows Maximilian (in a reverse shot that breaks the 180-degree rule, which forbids cutting to a shot from the opposite direction) suddenly getting angry, upsetting the table, then quickly apologizing. No explanation for this outburst, reductive or otherwise, is offered. In a later fragment (35), we hear him being berated mercilessly by his unseen table-tennis coach while they watch the video of his practice match with the machine. (Perhaps Haneke is indirectly giving us more explanation for Maximilian's final "inexplicable" act than he lets on.)

The final appearance of the fragmented cross motif comes in fragment 48, when we see its solution being attempted on a computer screen. The students then play pick-up sticks, which we watch in a beautiful overhead shot that emphasizes the sticks as a kind of abstract art image, and the other student explains to Maximilian B. that it is an example of skill against chance—"Geschicklichkeit" against "Zufall." This opposition seems intended to replicate or mirror that of Haneke's artistic "skill" in this film, which is being employed as a counter to the random "chance" of the universe.

The final section of the film, which begins, significantly, with the newscast of December 23, 1993, moves very quickly indeed, and most of the fragments are quite short. The kind woman, trying to teach German words to the Romanian boy, is juxtaposed with the inhuman technology that now seems ubiquitous in the film and is in fact found everywhere in contemporary society. This juxtaposition may have originally occurred to Haneke during his youthful studies of the German philosopher Martin

Heidegger (see Heidegger's important essay "The Question Concerning Technology"). There are quite immediate causes of Maximilian's immense frustration—when he is unable to pay for his gasoline because the cashier will only accept cash, yet the bank's ATM doesn't work and no one will allow him to go to the front of the bank line, even though his car is blocking traffic—yet the suggestion stands that a more general overreliance on the technology that has replaced human communication is equally, and more globally, to blame.

Throughout the film, the media, as the chief purveyor of noncommunication in our dysfunctional society, comes in for its usual richly deserved drubbing. Each of the five dates in the chronology commences with a televised news report, usually of some atrocity or another, often one connected with the war in Bosnia. Sometimes a critique of American foreign policy is strongly implied, but this may be a subjective judgment on this critic's part. As in the earlier films, the empty, repetitive forms of the news flatten everything out, and Haneke underlines this operation by almost always ending a news fragment in the middle of a sentence, a choice that implies, among other things, that the news has no end and that its form can accept and transform any content. What is also implicitly criticized is the moral relativity that allows the worst human atrocity (Serbian ethnic cleansing, for example) to hold the same news value and command the same amount of attention as the event that follows on the newscast, the trial of the entertainer Michael Jackson. Interestingly, we see this "same" news sequence again at the end of the film, though this time the news of the bank slaughter in Vienna is effortlessly folded into the space between the reporting on the horrors of Sarajevo and the frivolity of Michael Jackson.

But it is not only the media that is at fault here, because even if the media produces this flattening effect in its representations, the atrocities being reported on have also actually occurred. In other words, an obvious point that Haneke is making here—but no less telling for being obvious—is that we have somehow ended up in a world in which torture, murder, and depravity are commonplace. (In fragment 26, which begins the chronological section of the film dated October 26, 1993, the news program expressly reports on stories in which unknown gunmen have entered various places and murdered random victims, at one point the Irish IRA, and at another the Kurdish PKK operating in Turkey.) If this is the way the world is now, the director also seems to be implying, then why are we so shocked when an anonymous middle-class student from a military academy suddenly breaks down and kills three innocent people and himself in a bank? After all, this same meaningless, random violence (perhaps "justified" by one political discourse or another) is simultaneously happening all over the world. Nevertheless, the news program at the end of the film, in its short report on the killings at the bank, once again labels them "inexplicable," shakes its head, and then moves on, without missing a beat, to Michael Jackson. Thus, while any human motivation is finally unknowable, a quick look around at our violent, often heartless and antihuman society, Haneke is suggesting, may give ample grounds for expecting the worst.

Haneke's most specific political critique, and apparently the genesis of the film, concerns the Romanian boy, who is followed from the very beginning (the second fragment) to the very end (the penultimate fragment), when we see him left alone in his foster mother's car while she enters the bank. In various fragments throughout the film, we see him eat out of garbage cans (in fragment 8, to the disdainful astonishment of some bourgeois Viennese), attempt to connect in fragment 32 with another apparently homeless boy playing on the opposite side of the tracks in the U-Bahn (while the anonymous voice of an unseen enforcer blares on the subway's PA system), inexpertly beg on a street full of luxury shops in fragment 27, and so on.

The director tells Toubiana that "this actually happened in Austria. There was a boy of that age who crossed the border illegally, alone. . . . It ended well because he got so much publicity that the authorities were forced to let a family adopt him so that he could stay. But we didn't talk about the hundreds who've been caught and sent back. This boy's story . . . is what gave me the idea to make this film." (He says in a later interview that the Romanian boy was also the origin of his next film, *Code Unknown,* which deals largely with the problems of living in a pluralistic society.) Toubiana then astutely points out that the boy steals a comic book, which is naturally full of images, and then a camera, with which he makes more images. Haneke replies, "He's learned that in this society there's only the beauty of false images. It's only natural for him to adapt to that, to participate in this fantastic lie."

But these images, while perhaps false, can also be gorgeous, especially the ones that Haneke constructs in his role as filmmaker. Like Antonioni, Haneke often invests his energies in the creation of a formal visual beauty, apparently for its own sake, that relies on abstraction rather than figuration for its power. Thus, some of the opening fragments (2 and 3) use the familiar blue-black of his earlier films to offer an abstract aesthetic vision that is not (yet) tied to a narrative chain or a chronology. The most visually powerful fragment is 43, when the bank guard, alone in his bedroom at night, is plunged into the blue-black darkness, while the camera lovingly embraces the abstract patterns found on the window and the light fixture. Other beautiful, equally abstract shots occur with the pick-up sticks in fragment 48 and, more problematically, with the exquisitely seeping blood from the body of the dying or dead bank guard, accompanied by total silence, in fragment 68.

This apparently purposeful emphasis on the beauty of these images could put Haneke into a moral-aesthetic bind, for is he not merely adding to the exaltation of the image over reality? But his argument is not with images per se, since the world's greatest art, which he reveres, is itself composed of images. In our society, most images, especially of violence, have been constructed to be *consumable* rather than arresting objects of contemplation or irritation that resist easy acceptance. This is why he calls them "lies" and why he objects to mainstream cinema: "Even the most detestable side of things is made consumable. You see very violent films, and the violence is shown in a way that is very enjoyable. I find that disgusting" (Toubiana interview).

In any case, Haneke's final take on what he is about may be surprising to some, especially those who have subjected him to simplistic attacks. For it turns out that the (in)famous indirection of his method is a conscious strategy that leads to a rather touchingly old-fashioned exaltation of the redemptive power of art. Nevertheless, despite his usually convincing placement among the modernists, who still believed in high art, there is a decided streak of postmodernist sensibility in his thinking as well, one that has not been stressed enough, especially about the final impossibility of encountering truth. He seems to be expressing a fear about all image making and representation in general, including his own. Haneke's remarks to Toubiana on this subject deserve quoting at length, because they apply equally well to all of his films:

I think you also feel beauty and grace or what you will in the way you avoid showing it. There's a metaphysical side: today, if I tried to show beauty, it would immediately become a lie. By avoiding showing it, we can provoke it in the viewer's reactions.

There's a phrase from Adorno that I love. "Art is magic without the lie of being true." . . . I often wonder why I feel so happy when I'm confronted by a work of art. Especially with music, but also with literature or a film. Life without art is unimaginable to me. And what is it that makes you so happy? That's a difficult question to answer because in an age when God no longer exists, the desire for another world is still there. I don't mean desire for heaven, but for another image of the world. And I think you can only evoke it in avoiding showing it, because [otherwise] it immediately becomes banal.

If you force the desire toward that [on the viewer] by pointing your finger at all the false points, that's the best way to evoke it. . . . I'm not religious—but what is religion? I'm not a practicing Catholic, but naturally my films are the expression of a desire for a better world. That's normal, I think.

The showable part of the world is very dark. You can't show the mysterious side. Only in the spaces between realities. The moment you take hold of beauty, it disappears. Beauty is a grace; it happens. It's the concretization of the spirit. It's only in these spaces left by reality that it can find a concrete expression. The duty of art, in all forms, is to cultivate the desire for that, which is the most beautiful thing that exists.

Funny Games (1997)

The first, German-language version of *Funny Games* begins with a signature Haneke shot: a totally symmetrical, overhead, exceptionally distanced view of an unknown car on a nondescript freeway. On the sound track, an operatic aria can be heard at full volume. Then clearly middle-class voices—belonging to as yet unseen individuals—start, anonymously, guessing at the names of the singers. From the very beginning, Haneke employs opera as a symbolic shorthand for what the French sociologist Pierre Bourdieu would call "cultural capital": those intellectual and artistic accoutrements that mark the upper middle class.

The voices continue to guess the identities of the singers, establishing the idea of the *game*, which will become a central motif in the film (as we saw in *71 Fragments*, a game is a confluence of skill and chance), while the camera cuts to a closer, angled shot of the car on a two-lane road. No faces have yet appeared, allowing Haneke to withhold and thus play (his own little game) with audience identification, which will turn out to be one of his central concerns in this film.

The next cut is to another overhead shot, but this time it's much tighter, a close-up on the CD jewel cases of the operas these people carry in their car—a shot similar to those we have seen, especially of cash registers, in the three previous films. The camera then moves back to the overhead shot on the two-lane road, but we still see no faces and continue to hear only their guessing game being played. Then a side shot, closer to the car, which is pulling a boat, and finally we are rewarded with a frontal three-shot of the nuclear family, emphasizing its life-in-death artificiality, as in *The Seventh Continent*.

They are all benevolently smiling at one another, soundless and serene, and then suddenly the title "FUNNY GAMES" appears in giant red letters, like "BENNY'S VIDEO" at the beginning of that film. Now, however, the screamingly red title is accompanied by surprisingly bombastic, aggressive punk music by John Zorn that destroys all traces of the fragile opera arias the family and we have been listening to. It is as though this innocent bourgeois family—and we innocents in the audience—have suddenly been taken over, dominated, and even raped by a violence that lurks just outside, or just below, the comfortable world we think we inhabit.

Importantly, the music that cacophonously accompanies the title and that will appear twice more in the film—in the middle and at the end—is not only loud and assaultive, like a lot of punk rock, but nearly berserk, even insane. As such, it provides a complete counterpoint to all that we have heard and, by implication, what we have seen throughout the credits thus far.[3] It is the psychological, geometrical opposite of the operatic arias in a hundred different ways, and it is brilliantly juxtaposed with the simple faces that remain before us. This music—and a whole lot more—is going to "happen" to them, as it were, and these innocents haven't a clue.

The credits continue to roll against another side shot of the car and the close-up of the CD player, with accompanying close-ups on each of their smiling, contented faces. The juxtaposition of the peaceful visual track and the ultra-intense sound track is a powerful one. After Michael Haneke's name disappears at the end of the credits, the music suddenly stops, and this unnamed middle-class family quietly pulls up in front of a locked gate—a gate intended to protect and isolate the bourgeoisie from life's terrors, but which later becomes an obstacle to escape from these very terrors.

Things seem out of kilter to this family, and to us, from the very beginning, but nothing definite presents itself. Haneke again shows how well he *could* make a straightforward Hollywood genre film if that's what he wanted to do, as a deliberate, growing sense of dread and anxiety is masterfully established.

Even though we have already seen the faces of this upstanding family, unlike in the earlier films, much of the busy work of the putting away of food and so on is done in the usual Haneke manner of the close-up on the material object that simultaneously emphasizes its anonymity and its intense facticity as commodity, in the Marxist sense in which the *human* aspect of its production is erased. In other words, things as things predominate.

The imposition of power over the family, through a gradual insinuation of terror, begins with the apparently innocent desire of Peter, or "Fatty" (Frank Giering; he is called by various names in the film—yet one more little game), to borrow some eggs for the next-door neighbors whom he and his friend Paul (Arno Frisch) are ostensibly staying with. Paul has come over to help Georg (Ulrich Mühe; another lead character generically named Georg, and there will be more to come), the just-arrived husband, put his boat in the water. In a self-conscious nod to genre convention, the family's dog begins barking immediately, since pets and other animals are not bound by the polite niceties of social rules and obligations and, as the movies have taught us, have an instinctive sense of evil. Despite the bucolic scenes of the sailboat being put into the lake, the sense of dread, originally aroused by the violent punk music, lingers.

The eggs, especially when they are broken in several different scenes in the film, introduce a motif of viscera that also occasionally appears in *The Seventh Continent* (the eye exam), despite its primary emphasis, shared with *71 Fragments*, on a cold and color-drenched objecthood. Even in the very beginning, Anna (Susanne Lothar, in a magnificent, self-sacrificing performance) is seen cutting up an improbably large piece of meat—while talking on the telephone—that can't help but call attention to the guts and blood of our lives that usually remain carefully concealed from delicate middle-class sensibilities. This meat is not really a *symbol* of anything specific but rather signifies the gross presence of what Jacques Lacan might call the Real, the substratum that underlies the symbolic coding that is understood as reality in any given culture. Similarly, the victims are soon reduced to the abject level of cunning animals, intent solely on survival, the polar opposite of their refined life that the film opens with.

A related and equally important motif of communication first appears when Peter intentionally drops Anna's mobile phone into the water, and a great deal of time, now and later in the film, is spent trying to dry it in order to establish contact with the outside world. Obviously, this works first and foremost on the level of the genre plot—it's perhaps the modern equivalent of cutting the telephone wires leading to the house—but it also has implications for a favorite Haneke theme, the attenuation of the authenticity and humanity of modern life caused by increasing technology, especially that relating to the contemporary media and its promise of "enhanced" communication.

Slowly Paul and Peter insinuate themselves into the house by relying on the family's reluctance to be impolite. Hearing the dog continuing to bark, Anna says that it merely wants to *play*, and Peter remarks, "Nice funny game!" Paul then rudely pushes himself forward and begins playing with the golf clubs ("Would it be cheeky of me?" he faux-politely asks as he goes outside, ostensibly to try out the clubs), and soon enough silence ominously replaces the dog's barking. Anna finally breaks through the bourgeois social code and bluntly says, "I don't know what kind of game you are playing, but I am not playing it with you." Peter, who is now being called Tom, pretends to take offense at being accused of "playing a game."

As Haneke explains this moment to Toubiana in their interview on the DVD, it's "the anxiety of being faced with someone who doesn't react at all the way you're supposed to in this society where you respect the untouchability of the other, because that's a fundamental trust. If you've lost that, you're really lost." Interestingly, though, it's Anna who first breeches the powerful if usually unspoken division between the

Figure 6. Georg (Ulrich Mühe) tries to
reason with Paul (Arno Frisch) and Peter
(Frank Giering) in *Funny Games.*

social/intellectual niceties and the physical/corporeal/visceral when she
violently tries to pull Peter/Tom out the door. Similarly, it is her husband
Georg who attempts to deal with the situation rationally as a counter to
his wife's emotional response. Ironically, this liberal, enlightened desire
to play rational "arbitrator," as he calls it, rather than giving vent to an
unthinking, atavistic drive to protect the family at all costs, precipitates
their ordeal.

When Peter and Paul react by breaking his leg with one of his golf
clubs—the Freudian overtones seem obvious but remain unemphasized
by the director—Haneke is careful not to *show* them hitting Georg; we
hear the violence, and we see, throughout the entire length of the film,
its consequences. Thus, while it is true that we rarely *see* the actual blows
in this or any other Haneke film, we are forced constantly to confront the
victim's pain that results, a situation that produces a complicated dynamic
and belies the simplistic claim that virtually all violence in Haneke's films
is offscreen, hence nonexploitative. Clearly, the violence is being "represented," even if it is not actually "seen."

However, Haneke is also right when he maintains that, by refusing to
allow us an easy identification with the perpetrator of the violence, he is
not following the visual logic of most Hollywood films that feature good-

guy protagonists who use violence nonstop. Like Arnold Schwarzenegger in many of his action films, Peter and Paul are in control, but their cause is unjust and cruel, and hence impossible to support. Haneke forces us to identify with the receiver of the violence, the "innocent" bourgeois nuclear family, and thus to appreciate the horrifying nature of real violence rather than making it "consumable" and thus further anesthetizing us to it. In this way, the film is similar to a New Zealand film that made a medium-sized splash on the U.S. art-film circuit, *Once Were Warriors* (dir. Lee Tamahori, 1994). Here, the audience is positioned, visually and psychologically, to identify with the battered wife who is the object of the violence of her drunken Maori husband, and many viewers in the two screenings I attended were so deeply disturbed by the film that they were compelled to leave.

Nevertheless, in all the violence that is to come in *Funny Games*, it must also be tempting for at least some members of the audience to identify with the killers, simply because, even if they are cruel and unlikeable, they wield power and initiate all activity. Haneke puts audience identification into *play*, as it were, like so much else in this film, oscillating between the various poles of empathy and attachment that are being offered, simply to problematize the whole notion of identification and to begin to make viewers understand just what is happening when they make the apparently simple decision to watch a movie, especially a violent one.

There is another aspect to this displacement of identification that has to do with Haneke's complex and perhaps questionable ideas about guilt. As the director tells Cieutat and Rouyer in an interview translated for this volume, "The theme of guilt is present in all my films. *Funny Games* was meant as a metaphor for a society that has turned inward and excluded the exterior world. Men today live in prisons they've created for themselves. They can't escape, because they're the ones that built the walls that surround them. So it's their own fault. This is where the feeling of guilt that every victim feels comes from. There is no victim in my films who is completely innocent. But nevertheless these victims aren't killed because of their guilty feelings." This last concession is a welcome one, but Haneke's seeming insistence on some kind of moral equivalence between the family's "guilt" and that of Peter and Paul appears excessive, if not ridiculous.

There's more. "In *Funny Games*," the director continues, "I was playing with an ironic contradiction: each one of my victims became guilty of a reprehensible act before the torturers took over. Of course, they were forced by the two young men to act that way, like the mother who suddenly isn't polite any longer, the father who slaps one of the young men, or the son who was the first to shoot. It was an ironic way of keeping spectators from siding with the victims right away because they sympathized completely with them. I was also trying to draw the attention of the audience to the fact—in terms of criminal violence—that things in the world aren't so simple. Obviously, there's no connection between the guilt of these people and their final disappearance. It's not some kind of punishment. It would be completely idiotic to think that." But perhaps it is also somewhat idiotic to think that these ultimately innocent victims, merely by defending themselves against such vicious evildoers, "became guilty of a reprehensible act before the torturers took over" to the point that we would begin to realize "in terms of criminal violence—that things in the world aren't so simple."

The motif of the game comes back in the form of playacting (forcing Georg to imitate the voice of a ship's captain, for example) and in Paul's proposal of a guessing game of "Hot and Cold" to torment them further, psychologically at least, regarding the fate of the dog. It is at this moment that Haneke begins what is probably the most experimental set of gestures undertaken in any of his films. Right in the middle of the game, Paul turns and gives a big wink to the camera and thus, by implication, to the audience. (Theoretically, he could be winking at an unseen Peter, but this would make Peter an unpleasant and unwanted stand-in for us, in our physical and emotional position, adding to our discomfort.) It is a long shot, with the entire field in relatively sharp focus, but with Paul in the front of the shot in extreme close-up. Here most people will think, visually at least, of Stanley Kubrick's 1971 film *A Clockwork Orange*.

Such self-reflexive, quasi-Brechtian moments increase as the film proceeds. Unlike most directors who have employed such a technique, Haneke seems intent on using it to implicate the audience, emotionally and psychologically, in what is going on rather than to reveal, for aesthetic or political reasons (as with Brecht), the make-believe, manufactured nature of the ultra-realist proceedings. Whether this device actually achieves Haneke's goal is another matter.

Haneke openly admits his polemical intention: "The film must be unsettling. It's the only film I made to provoke. People have often criticized me for making films just to provoke. That was never the case. But in this film, yes. It made me happy to give an awakening kind of slap: Look at what you normally watch!" (Toubiana interview).

He is also clear, and clearly didactic, about his intentions regarding the act of spectatorship. "The killer communicates with the viewer. That means he makes him his accomplice. I'm making the viewer the accomplice of the killer, and ultimately I'm reproaching him for this position. It's a little sarcastic, but I wanted to show how you always end up the accomplice of the killer if you watch this kind of film. Not in a self-reflexive film like this one, but in films that show violence in an acceptable way. We always know that violence is taking place, that it's consumable, and we don't realize that we're accomplices to this. That's what I wanted to show" (Toubiana interview). This argument frankly seems very confused. For one thing, when Haneke says, "I'm making the viewer the accomplice of the killer, and ultimately I'm reproaching him for this position," it's like saying, "I handed my car keys to the criminal, and I'm reproaching him for stealing my car." There's a logical inconsistency: at one point, Haneke claims that the direct address to the viewer makes him or her a de facto "accomplice," but he immediately follows that by claiming that this does *not* happen "in a self-reflexive film like this one."

But to what extent *could* any self-reflexive gesture, an address directly to the audience, ever imply a collaboration between audience and killer? For one thing, the self-reflexivity, by definition, immediately indicates that what is going on is *playacting*, not real violence, so what exactly can the audience ever be guilty of if it knows that everything is fake? Furthermore, how can this new "knowledge" be transferable to a non-self-reflexive violent film, the kind that Haneke disapproves of?

The distinction Haneke wants to make is more clearly articulated in another interview, in which he compares *Funny Games* to Oliver Stone's *Natural Born Killers* (1994). "My goal was a kind of counter-program to *Natural Born Killers*. In my view, Oliver Stone's film, and I use it only as an example, is the attempt to use a fascist aesthetic to achieve an anti-fascist goal, and this doesn't work. What is accomplished is something like the opposite, since what is produced is something like a cult film where the montage style complements the violence represented and presents it largely in a positive light. . . . *NBK* makes the violent image alluring while allowing no space for the viewer. I feel this would be very difficult to argue about *Funny Games*. *Benny's Video* and *Funny Games* are different kinds of obscenity, in the sense that I intended a slap in the face and a provocation" (Sharrett).[4]

Even though Haneke seems to have an unambiguous and untroubled view of what he is doing, it is legitimate to entertain doubts about the entire enterprise. Thus, as Haneke tells Toubiana, "The pleasure is to show the viewer how manipulatable he is . . . and I think it works well in the movie. Even though I always give the viewer new opportunities to escape. . . . I've always said it's a film that you watch if you need this film. If you don't need this film, you leave. If someone stays until the end, he needed to be tortured during that time to understand. If you want to, you can understand very quickly. It seems hypocritical to me for someone to watch the film to the end and afterward protest and say, 'You can't do that.' I say, 'Then why did you stay? Obviously, you wanted to know, you wanted to feel all this until the end.'"

This whole line of analysis strikes me as more than a bit disingenuous, since all sorts of other factors—social (will your friends leave too?), the pull of a narrative, an interest in "figuring out what's going on," curiosity about how far Haneke is willing to go, even the refusal to lose the money spent on a ticket!—might keep a viewer in his or her seat. A decision to continue watching a film can be made for many reasons besides "needing to be tortured."

In any case, the self-reflexivity quickly gets caught up and intertwined with the game motif and becomes the film's central game. Another game includes Paul making up a story of Peter's deprived childhood, then mocking the presumed bleeding-heart liberals who would blame the killers' actions on society's shortcomings. As Paul puts it, "Do you really think he comes from a deprived background? He's a spoiled little shitface tormented by ennui and world-weariness, weighed down by the weight of existence."

For his part, Georg continues to cling to reason by continually asking them *why* they are doing what they are doing, but of course he never gets a rational answer beyond the obviously bogus one that they are "drug addicts," another mockery of liberal explanations for sociopathic behavior. Haneke seems ultimately to suggest that there simply *is* no good reason for them to be torturing people, just as there was no good reason for the family in *The Seventh Continent* to destroy their property and themselves, for Benny to kill the girl, or for the cadet to go berserk in the bank. As the director tells Toubiana, "I read lots of articles, especially after *Benny's Video*, about criminal acts committed by young people, always young people from good families, so without any social explanation. Always from families more or less bourgeois who committed crimes neither for revenge or to get rich, only for the pleasure of feeling a sensation. That really disturbed me. And that was in a way the trigger for the story."

Because their motives are unpredictable, they become even more frightening. In this, they relate back to the "motives," less successfully dramatized, of the title character of *Benny's Video*. Peter and Paul seem to be into this for its own sake, for the sheer thrill of it, and they give no thought to the traditional bourgeois notion of delayed or sublimated gratification, nor do they allow their irrational pleasure to be hampered by inconvenient ethical rules that the middle class finds indispensable.

Paul's next idea for a game is betting on the time of death of each one of the family members, and when their astonishment is shown in individual close-ups, Paul turns to the camera and directly addresses the audience, as he did earlier, but now with specific questions: "What do you think? Do you think they've a chance of winning? You are on their side, aren't you? So, who will you bet with?" While this intervention has the Brechtian effect of alerting us to the fiction of what we're watching, it hardly seems to morally implicate us in anything.

The killers then pretend to realize suddenly that the family will lose in any case. "As they say on television: 'The bets are placed!'" Later, when Anna asks, "Why don't you just kill us right away?" Paul's reply, sarcastically seconding Haneke's critique of Hollywood, is, "Don't forget the entertainment value. We'd all be deprived of our pleasure."

They next want to play a sick game called "Kitten in the Bag," which they describe as "a nice game, a family game," while slapping the child (Georgie) around. The child's humanity is obscured when a hood is pulled over his head, just as the humanity of the entire family has been metaphorically ravaged by these arbitrary games the killers insist on playing. Also, the parents seem finally to break through social conven-

Figure 7. Paul (Arno Frisch)
wants to play a game with Georgie
(Stefan Clapczynski) in *Funny Games*.

tion in the intensity of their atavistic desire/need to protect the child who, alas, is the first to die.

The most charged games in the world, of course, involve sexuality, and this is also the case in *Funny Games* when the killers insist that Georg ask Anna to take her clothes off. Again, though, it's not really sexuality that they're interested in but the fact of her nudity, and thus her human vulnerability at its most basic level. It's important to note that Haneke carefully avoids showing Anna in a nude state. (But we know that she is naked, of course, and her *humiliation* is visible in her face and body language—hence a variation of the dynamic regarding the showing or not-showing of violence seems to be at work.) Georg, her emasculated husband, is also unable to look, and Haneke gives us instead a series of close-ups on heads: Anna, Peter, Anna, Georgie, Anna. In formal visual terms, these discrete, quick close-ups contrast powerfully with the single extreme long-take (which lasts over ten minutes), in long shot, which is about to come.

Another psychological weapon in Paul's arsenal is language. In his hands, or rather in his mouth, Paul's nonstop, ultra-juridical, hyper-"logical" verbiage becomes a tool of offense, especially in light of the reticence and spareness of dialogue in Haneke's earlier films. Perhaps as a nod to the German theorists Max Horkheimer and Theodor Adorno's *Dialectic of Enlightenment*, which Haneke surely read as a philosophy student, we understand in the person of Paul the theory of the utterly irrational outbreak—for Horkheimer and Adorno, the Nazis and the Holocaust—not as an outgrowth or intensification of irrationality but as a product of the *ultra-rational*, inherited from the Enlightenment, that disregards all purely human, nonlogical values.[5]

At this point in the film, more self-conscious genre conventions begin to be employed. In other words, *Funny Games* finally allows itself to begin to resemble films that we have seen before and that Haneke is angry at us for having enjoyed. Though its plot is still ultra-minimalist, it feels more story-driven, compared with the barely visible, microscopic narrative threads of the director's earlier films, and certainly much more like a conventional thriller. One common genre motif is the protective device—in this case, the outer gates—that ironically turns against those it is meant to protect. Georgie's escape attempt is first stymied by the locked gates, originally meant to keep evil out; when he gives up and runs to a neighboring house for safety, a motion sensor, installed to prevent criminal activity, suddenly turns all the outdoor lights on, revealing his location to the criminals. When he gets to the house, he discovers the dead body of a female playmate (though Haneke treats this in the most shorthand manner possible, barely indicating, in a cluttered long shot, her legs sticking out from behind a wall). While Paul hunts him down in classic genre fashion, much of what we see, again classically, is from the subjective-camera viewpoint of Georgie. Next a gun is revealed, though, perhaps as a joke on Chekhov, nothing is ever done with it. It is at this point that Paul puts a CD in the player, and the violent punk music of John Zorn reappears with a vengeance.

Back in the family's summer house, Peter is flipping through television channels. At first, the scene seems like a parody of normal middle-class life, with the woman sitting silently on the sofa. Haneke again turns to the audio track for his dissonance, in this case the horribly grating sounds of a Formula One automobile race that is so offensive—to Anna's ears and ours—that, later in the film, after she laboriously escapes her bonds, the first thing she struggles to do, still hobbled, is turn off the TV.

The killers go into a riff on Beavis and Butthead, and it's hard to know whether Haneke is being facile here (in the United States, at the time the film was made, Beavis and Butthead were often considered by hectoring commentators to be the nadir of popular culture, a clear sign of the impending collapse of Western Civilization) or merely trying to illustrate the ubiquity of global (American) television culture. Similarly, when they decide to kill Georgie, the violence occurs offscreen, and blood spurts all over the TV screen. (Is the violence therefore still offscreen?) This could possibly be recuperated in a number of ways: as simple "realism"; as graphically striking, in terms of its abstract lines; as facilely gory; or as a rather ham-handed satire of the Hollywood thriller genre.

A version of "Eeny, Meeny, Miney, Moe," another game, will decide who is killed first. Paul, demonstrating his complete amorality, nonchalantly continues to make his sandwich in the kitchen while hearing unspecified violence in the other room, similar to the distanciation operated by the same actor in *Benny's Video* while the dead girl's body lies on the floor. All the while, of course, we continue to hear the lacerating aural violence of the televised automobile race on the soundtrack, which meshes perfectly with the "real" violence we are also hearing.

Arbitrarily, like the games they've been playing, Peter and Paul suddenly announce that they are leaving. In a flash, they are gone. Perhaps this occurs because these figures are more symbolic—of pure Evil? or of the evils of contemporary society?—than real. In fact, Haneke, in the Sharrett interview, says revealingly that they aren't "really characters, they're artifacts." An amazingly long take, more than ten minutes in duration, begins, in extreme long shot, of the bound-up Anna, accompanied by the annoying sounds of the auto race. Apparently in shock, she is weirdly lit from below by an overturned lamp—and then she finally begins to move. We see Georg's leg sticking out on the left, and their child's dead body on the right. Once Anna is able to hobble over to the television to turn it off, the sudden quiet is overwhelming—to her and to us—and she remains for a long while almost absolutely stationary, presumably in shock, and still in long shot. It's as though after all the mayhem that has taken place, the camera wants to keep the audience at a remove, perhaps to give us a chance to recover before the next onslaught begins.

The camera pans with Anna as she hops out of the room, leaving as the central focus of the shot an apparently catatonic Georg, who suddenly begins to emit primal screams as if he is finally breaking down, or rather letting himself break down. Anna comes back into the frame to calm him. All becomes quiet once more, as Haneke again demonstrates his mastery of sound dynamics. One of the most difficult parts of the film comes next, as we watch Georg's tiny, excruciatingly painful steps toward escape.

The first cut arrives, more than ten minutes after this extraordinary long-take shot has begun, and takes us to an ironic shot of the outside of the apparently peaceful house. It is decided that Anna will seek help alone because Georg is too badly hurt. In a reprise of the communication motif, Georg spends an inordinate amount of wasted time trying to get the mobile phone to work. Despite all our gadgets for communication, Haneke seems to be saying, we remain unable to communicate and, ultimately, at the mercy of primal animal impulses. Much of what follows continues in the direction of genre conventions, but always well done. Some passionate words are exchanged between Anna and Georg in the midst of their suffering, transforming the simple scene into something emotionally devastating and real. It is as though they have been awakened, through this ordeal, to the most basic forms, and meanings, of human life.

The cruelest game that remains is perhaps the game of chance, as we saw in *71 Fragments*. On the road, Anna avoids hailing the first car that passes, fearing it contains the killers—but, of course, it turns out that this car would have saved her and Georg. Instead, she chooses the *second* car, which, by chance, as we learn later, does contain Peter and Paul, who have decided to return to wreak more mayhem. We return to the house, and in a brilliant Hitchcockian gesture, a frightened Georg hears a noise, then sees a golf ball rolling down the hallway. In English, the unseen Paul taunts, "Playtime again!"

Just as Georgie was earlier stripped of his humanity by having his head covered with the bag, Anna is now seen in a ghastly, quite upsetting pose with a rag rolled into a ball and stuck in her mouth. Georg is bloody, but Haneke has, as usual, chosen not to show us the beating itself. And then the arbitrary games begin all over again, with Paul insisting obsessively on the *rules*, even though they seem open to an infinity of interpretations according to the whims of the killers. Again, what comes to mind is Horkheimer and Adorno's thesis about the greatest, most inhumane irrationality proceeding directly from the most meticulous application of reason and its most common manifestation in human affairs, "the rules," which are always determined by those who hold the power. Haneke's own take on this dynamic of rules is similar, though expressed in a formal or dramaturgical light rather than a political one. As he says to Toubiana, "I told the family, you're playing the tragedy, and to the two others, you're playing the comedy. And when you put the two together, it's horrible because there are no more rules. The rules are different, and then you have a catastrophe which is essential." What results is a cacophony of different (im)moral frameworks.

At this point, the game is arbitrarily expanded to include *how* Georg and Anna will be killed. "We want to offer the audience something and show what we can do, right?" says Paul, with a self-reflexive smirk. "You can play again. We are going to play 'The Loving Wife,' or, 'Whether by knife or whether by gun / Losing your life can sometimes be fun.' You have to play with us." The new rules state that even though Georg has been chosen to be the next to be killed, Anna can decide to take his place. "Anna, have you had enough, or do you want to play some more?" one of them asks. When Georg suggests that she not answer, Paul responds, "Huh, that's cowardly. We're not up to feature-film length yet," as he looks directly at the camera and the audience, asking, "Is that enough? But you want a real ending, with plausible plot development, don't you?" Again, one wonders what effect this gesture has on an audience.

Georg is next tortured with a little knife, but once again we only hear but do not see what is going on, which is more than enough. "Anna, you only need to follow the rules to avoid all this," they taunt. Then they force her to flawlessly recite, from memory, a childhood prayer to God to save her husband from further torture.[6]

At this moment comes Haneke's most overt (and most innovative) self-reflexive gesture. Suddenly, Anna grabs the gun and shoots Peter full in the chest. Paul knocks her down and, screaming wildly for the remote control, stops the "film" we have been watching, as though it were all on television, and rewinds the scene we've just witnessed. In the second "version" of the scene, which we see next, when "play" is pressed, Paul, apparently in charge of the script as well as the rules and the remote, easily prevents her from obtaining the gun. Because she has "broken the rules," Paul tells her, Georg is shot dead, offscreen. In showing the two versions of the scene, audience desire—that the family be saved—is overtly acknowledged and then cruelly denied. It's also the most completely (and purposely) "artificial" moment in this mostly realistic film.

For Haneke, this is the supreme gesture of overt audience manipulation, undertaken to make us aware of how most films manipulate us surreptitiously. "It's the top in this system of breaking the illusion. Before, as well, when the character speaks to the viewer, it's a moment where you completely lose your reference point. You're not in the story anymore, but at the same time you remain in the story because the character remains. And there are several stages of alienation, and that's the height of this system, the rewinding of the scene" (Toubiana interview).

Yet, for all his finger wagging, Haneke is not naive about the question of manipulation, realizing that it is inherent to the viewing process. Thus, as he tells Cieutat and Rouyer, "With no matter what film, you're being manipulated, but people are dishonest enough never to say it. I, on the other hand, show it to say it. I think it's the exact opposite position. You can't escape this problematic: as soon as you make a frame, it's already a manipulation. I just try to do it in a transparent manner."

We next cut to Peter, Paul, and Anna, in bright yellow rain slickers, preparing to go out on the lake in the family's boat. Peter begins talking philosophical nonsense that seems, at least at first, to be something to take seriously: "The problem is not only getting from the world of antimatter to reality, but also to regain communication," and so forth, but we quickly realize that this is gibberish, as arbitrary and meaningless as anything else these two have proposed during the course of the film. (Is Haneke making proleptic fun of the critics' explanations of his film before they are written?) At a certain moment, the bound Anna is simply pushed over the side of the boat with a cheery "Ciao, bella!" Paul explains that he killed her earlier than planned because it was too difficult sailing with her and because he was getting hungry.

The two laugh a little like Beavis and Butthead and then continue their "philosophical" discussion. Peter speaks of cyberspace, arguing that one universe is real, while the other is fiction. "And where is your hero now, in reality or in fiction?" asks Paul. Peter replies, "His family is in reality, and he's in fiction." Paul: "But the fiction is real, isn't it?" Peter: "How do you mean?" Paul: "Well, you see it in the film, right?"

Peter: "Of course." Paul: "So, it's just as real as the reality which we see likewise, right?" Peter: "Crap." Paul: "How so?"

Paul is of course correct that the profilmic scene that is being acted and shot is real in its own way, even if it has a simultaneous life as a representation of something else. The representation—in other words, the film that we are watching—is also "real." The two terms thus easily collapse, as Haneke continues his own little game—via the mouths of these men who may not even be characters but only "artifacts"—about the final inseparability of reality and fiction.

And then everything starts all over again, in a sense, at the house of Georg and Anna's neighbor, except that it's now Paul borrowing the eggs. The film ends with Paul looking right at the camera/audience—in a shot that is startlingly reminiscent of the poster for *A Clockwork Orange*— acknowledging and forcing us to acknowledge, at least in Haneke's view, our full participation in what has just transpired. Suddenly, John Zorn's upsetting punk music starts again, for the third and final time. Freeze frame, then: "FUNNY GAMES," in the familiar bright red letters, followed by the credits over the music. As the light comes up on Paul's unsmiling face, previously shadowed, we begin to see it more clearly, and how clearly determined it remains.

At the film's world premiere at the Cannes Film Festival in 1997, it elicited exactly the kind of mixed response that Haneke was apparently looking for: "At Cannes, it was a total mess. Some hated it, and some loved it, and that gave me proof that it was working as I'd intended. When she shot the fat guy [in the first version of the notorious scene that Paul rewinds on the remote], people started clapping. When it was rewound, there was total silence, because they understood that they had let themselves be totally manipulated. Because they had applauded a murder. That's what I wanted to show, and that worked very well" (Toubiana interview).

Haneke's analysis seems facile here, if not downright silly, since this obvious instance of self-defense on the part of Anna—she and her husband have been tortured for hours, and their son has been brutally slaughtered and his brains spattered on the living-room television—can hardly be labeled a "murder" that the audience is applauding. Of course, we clap when justice, however "primitive" a form it may take, seems to be accomplished.

Haneke also tells Toubiana that he told his producer at the time of the premiere that "if the film became a big success, it would be because it was also misunderstood. It has been big on DVD in English-speaking countries. The representation of violence has evolved, the shock of this film has become less, and now I'm afraid that the violence in this film has also become consumable." However, as we shall see when we now take a brief look at Haneke's English-language, shot-by-shot remake of the film, which came out in March 2008,[7] the director need not have worried overmuch about the film's success in English-speaking countries. The American version was a resounding flop in the United States, grossing less than 1.3 million dollars.

Funny Games (U.S.; 2007–8)

For reasons that remain unclear,[8] ten years after the release of the original *Funny Games*, Haneke chose, as his first project in English, to remake it, virtually shot by shot and line by line, with the well-known international actors Naomi Watts and Tim Roth. Since it would be unbearably cruel to expect a critic-scholar to actually compare the two films shot by shot and line by line, I ask the reader to take it on faith in the following brief discussion that while some rather large differences are evident—it's set in the Hamptons, not Austria; it's in English, not German; and all the actors are different—for the most part its structure and mechanics remain identical.

The opening overhead shots of the car, during the credits, are the same, as is the plethora of extreme long shots and close-ups of hands and other body parts before faces are revealed. The bursting-through of the screaming punk music as the title covers the screen in bright red letters is still there, as is the juxtaposition of the smiling, innocent family and the discordant sound track, giving us a foretaste of the mayhem to come. The tracking shots, the gates, the long stationary shots on the big dark houses between takes, the white gloves the evildoers wear, the strange, artificial formality of the language, the emphasis on game playing, the self-reflexive asides (including lines like "you shouldn't forget the importance of entertainment"), the rewind of the repressed scene—all remain, virtually unchanged. A tiny, probably insignificant difference resides in the use of the word "awesome" by the nefarious pair, which thus becomes a kind of signifier of the new, American version. Peter (a.k.a. Fatty and Tom) is now more appropriately known as "Tubby."

Of course, as the French philosopher Jacques Derrida taught us long ago, no two things can ever be truly identical or the *same,* since at the very least they will always occupy two different spaces and times. The first major difference showed up in the impossible marketing position that Warner Independent Pictures, the film's distributor in America, was placed in during the film's commercial run in the United States between March and May of 2008. Apparently, a more mainstream audience was envisioned for the remake, an audience looking to see a thriller—which, according to the director's statements, was exactly the ideal, the impossible audience that he had sought from the beginning. In other words, an audience whom he could chastise for liking the kind of film that he was proposing they buy tickets to see.

Despite being in English and set in the Hamptons, it's obvious that the film is too idiosyncratic and still bears too many traces of its art-house origins (the various self-reflexive gestures are still in place, as well as the long-takes in which "nothing happens") to ever attract a mass U.S. audience. While self-reflexivity can work in genre films, as in Wes Craven's *Scream* series, it really works only when it's meant to be funny. At the same time, the American version's overt fascination with and depiction of violence (whether disguised as an accusatory investigation of audience response or not) is precisely the kind of the thing that would keep most art-film lovers away.

Though camera angles, camera distance, and the mise-en-scène are virtually identical in the two versions, two moments of technique are different, one small and one large. The small thing is that when John Zorn's punk-rock music suddenly blares in the middle of things (once at the beginning of the film, when it forces out the classical music they are listening to in the car; once when Paul is looking for young Georgie in the house next door; and once at the end), in the American version it still blares, but it's noticeably less loud and consequently less disturbing. Similarly, the voiceover of the announcer in the NASCAR races on television is much less viscerally annoying than in the German version, though the first thing that Ann (Naomi Watts) does during the famous extreme long-take scene (when they think the bad guys have gone) is, once again, to turn off the TV. It is difficult to tell whether this was meant as a kind of superficial domestication of the film, and whether it was Haneke's choice or the distributor's.

The bigger thing is at once simple and powerful: the film is in English and thus seems to be more directly accessible to the American consciousness. But is this really the case? Clearly, it would be more accessible to the average mall-going viewer, unused to negotiating subtitles, and thus accessible to *more people*, at least in principle. But for a viewer who is used to watching foreign-language films and who has already seen the film in German, frankly, it's a bit of a bore, and certainly no more immediately frightening or upsetting because it's in English and stars the more familiar Naomi Watts. (In fact, the very presence of Watts, precisely because she's a star, tends to work against the frightening realism achieved in the original version.) The question that arose over and over in the mind of this viewer was, "Why was this remake ever undertaken in the first place?"

The acting is excellent, with professionals like Watts and Roth always completely convincing. Michael Pitt and Brady Corbet, with their fleshy, full-lipped features, may even be more effective producers of dread and anxiety than Otto Frisch and Frank Giering. Young Georgie (Devon Gearhart) seems like an adult and a child at the same time, a disturbing combination that fits the film's dynamics quite well.

On the important question of sexual vulnerability and nudity, it is true that Naomi Watts is also not shown in the nude, and the camera is at first very puritanical in her regard, even when she is most psychologically exposed. But then for a long stretch of time we do see her only in bra and panty briefs that prominently display her pubic bone and that finally seem to be much more revealing that the undergarments of Susanne Lothar in the original. This could be intentional on Haneke's part, to enhance the sexual quotient so that the audience will be more torn about taking (sexual) pleasure in the spectacle of someone being tortured—or not.

In any case, the film was greeted with, at best, mixed reviews when it first appeared in the United States in 2008. Receiving only a mediocre 50 percent rating on the well-known critics' Web site *Rotten Tomatoes*, it managed to upset quite a few well-known critics, such as Anthony Lane in the *New Yorker* and A. O. Scott in the *New York Times*, the headline of whose review reads, "A Vicious Attack on Innocent People, on the

Screen and in the Theater." David Edelstein's comments on National Public Radio can perhaps stand for the majority opinion: "It's difficult to grapple with serious themes when what comes through most vividly is the director's sadism. In the end, *Funny Games* is little more than hightoned torture porn with an edge of righteousness that's not unlike Peter and Paul's. . . . The movie is shallow and itself glacially unengaged—a punkish assault without punk's redeeming passion."

Code Unknown (2000)

With *Code Unknown,* the very Germanic sensibility of Michael Haneke makes an impressive leap into a very French world: Paris location, French-language script, and a well-known French actress, Juliette Binoche, who had expressed interest in working with the director. Based on the artistic success and even notoriety of his earlier German-language films, Haneke was able to obtain financing from Arté France Cinema, France 2 Cinema, and Canal+, as well as continuing German participation by Bavaria Film and, somewhat surprisingly, financial support from the Romanian government and a Romanian production company, owing to the primary location of one of the three stories that comprise the film.

The source of the title, according to the director, derives "from the first impression I had felt in Paris, that one couldn't go anywhere without knowing the code number of a building. And for me that was a very good first image in terms of the film's contents. Like the preface you find before beginning a novel that tells you that without the proper code, you won't be able to figure out the feelings you're going to be confronted with: you are going to stay outside, and there won't be any communication. So it's a title that has two meanings" (Cieutat interview in this volume).

I may be part of a critical minority in finding that while some of its themes and motifs are fascinating, *Code Unknown* is not wholly successful either dramatically (the acting is decidedly uneven) or narratively, given the basic problem that multistory films often have involving spectators emotionally in the lives of multiple characters. (The narratives of Haneke's earlier films are often incoherent, but purposely so, and to often superb effect.) Nor is the film as aesthetically or formally interesting as his earlier, more challenging films. Yet there is still quite a bit going on here, and Haneke's apparently conscious attempt to appeal to more mainstream art-house sensibilities, and to expand his international audience, should obviously not be condemned out of hand.

The film is broken down into a somewhat awkward arrangement of three different stories that only marginally interweave with one another. The first centers on Anne Laurent (Juliette Binoche), an actress living in Paris. The second concerns an African family living a disadvantaged life in the same city, and the third is about Maria (Luminita Gheorghiu), a Romanian woman reduced to begging in the streets before being picked up by the police and deported. If its fractious multicultural aspect has grown a bit stale, at the time of the film's appearance it was a serious French (and worldwide) social problem only beginning to come into focus; ongoing riots in the Parisian *banlieue* attest to Haneke's perceptiveness in this regard.

There is also quite a bit of that patented Haneke vagueness and ambiguity—enough to keep academic critics analytically engaged several decades into the future—those same qualities that will flower, and attain deeper resonance, in *Caché* (2005). Now, however, the ambiguity exists at the highest level of narrative and theme and no longer—or at least not quite as frequently—requires viewers to struggle to decipher the simplest relationships between characters, as in the earlier films.

The film begins with an Antonionian framing gesture that recalls, again, the strategy employed at the beginning of Antonioni's *L'Eclisse* (1962) about how this film is to be watched and interpreted. A perfectly framed long shot shows a young girl, who is deaf (as we will shortly discover), and who is increasingly jammed up against a blank white wall as she crouches into an ever smaller and more vulnerable bundle. Next, close-ups on individual children reveal that they are all "speaking" in sign language, which is, of course, to many viewers, a *code inconnu*.

They try to guess what the first girl is acting out, in her game of charades, and the absence of music or any other sounds, beyond the guttural tones often associated with the deaf and now generated occasionally by one of the children surrounding her, produces a strange effect. They are obviously desperate to communicate, unlike so many of the hearing characters we will meet in the film. The final interpretive suggestion made by one of the children is "imprisoned?" as we are notified in the subtitles. When the first girl shakes her head no, the title flashes on the screen, accompanied by a subtitle, "Récit incomplet de divers voyages" (Incomplete story of different journeys), and the name of the director.

We are then thrown immediately into the world of Anne Laurent and the precipitating incident that brings all of these different lives together. Anne's boyfriend is named Georges (Thierry Neuvic; yes, another Anne and Georges), a professional photographer who covers "zones of conflict." Georges's younger brother Jean (Alexandre Hamidi), fed up with the brutal life on the farm he shares with his father, has come to the city to stay with Anne and Georges, who is in Kosovo at the moment. The theme of the "unknown code" receives its first overt mention when Jean complains that he couldn't get into Anne's apartment building because "the fucking code has been changed." Throughout their mutually exasperating discussion, Haneke's camera follows them tightly in a heavily marked tracking shot, now to the right, now to the left. This tracking shot, with its host of expressive meanings, will become one of the signature techniques of all of Haneke's French-language films.

After being told by Anne that he can't stay, Jean moves back toward the left, with the camera suddenly reversing direction to follow him, until he comes across some young men playing guitars and singing. In a fit of frustration, he throws a bag, with a pastry Anne has bought him, now half-eaten, into the lap of Maria, the Romanian woman (whose identity we learn later), who occupies the lower left of the frame.

At this point, Amadou (Ona Yu Lenke), a young African man, accosts Jean and tries to force him to apologize to the woman he has disrespected. They struggle, and soon enough the French police, portrayed throughout as brutal and uncaring, hustle everyone off to jail and end up deporting Maria simply because she happened to be in the wrong place at the wrong time. In this fashion, the three interconnected stories are set into motion. What comes across most clearly in this initiating scene is the tension and ill-feeling that reigns in the contemporary multicultural urban space.

The long-duration tracking shot is also a long-take, a shooting style that Haneke has used since the beginning of his career. The director has said that it has several purposes in the film, some of which are related to one of his central artistic concerns, the manipulation of the audience. It also turns out that the technique is intended as a deliberate counter to the camerawork of the film-within-the-film that the actress Anne is shooting, yet the two opposing styles end up being not so different after all.

Figure 8. Anne (Juliette Binoche) watches
as Jean (Alexandre Hamidi) struggles
to escape the clutches of Amadou
(Ona Lu Yenke) in *Code Unknown*.

Haneke explains his use of the long-take to Michel Cieutat in the interview translated for this volume:

> I used the long-take . . . [f]irst, in order to find a rigid structure for the fragments, as in a puzzle, but also to separate them from the scenes relating to the film-within-the-film, which are shown in the usual way. Another reason was to let each scene develop in real time, which is a way of not manipulating time; which is also a kind of manipulation, because it's a question of showing that the scenes of the film-within-the-film are just as artificial as the other sequences. In fact, in *Code Unknown*, everything is related to manipulation. I play with that, because everyone knows that cinema is a manipulation of the spectator; and it's not a question of knowing it but of feeling it, of understanding it more deeply. Whence the difference in the way the two types of scenes were handled. . . . I also wanted to show, starting with these two opposed aesthetics, that spectators taken by a well-made story can be totally manipulated . . . as I wanted them to be!

In other words, Haneke uses the long-take to make us understand on a visceral level that we are being manipulated when we watch conventional cinema. But once this lesson has been learned, the next lesson is that we are always being manipulated by the long-take style—in fact, by any style—as well.

After the typical fade to black, which insists, as always, on the idea of *fragments* rather than on a developed narrative, the next scene introduces another favorite Haneke theme, the interrelation of politics, the news media, the depiction of various atrocities in different conflicted zones, and the power or usefulness of the visual image, a conflicted topos that has been a staple of his cinema from the beginning. What is perhaps new here, as hinted at in the previous quotation, is that he seems also to be implicating his *own* visual representation as part of the media landscape that is to be critiqued, in a way that goes beyond the somewhat smug and showy self-reflexivity of *Funny Games*.

In this vignette, we see a close-up of various unidentified war photographs, while on the sound track we hear Georges's voice reading aloud a more or less factual letter to Anne. Interestingly, though, after a while the content of the letter suddenly veers over into the personal while the visual track is still occupied by the horrific photographs, creating a disturbing, obviously intentional juxtaposition that begins to raise questions, albeit indistinct, about the relation of the personal and the political. While Georges is in the middle of a sentence, the camera cuts, once again, to black.

In the next scene, Haneke loads the dice a bit by focusing on an old black cab driver—only after the usual epistemological detective work that the director always insists we perform do we discover that he is Amadou's father—who gets a call informing him that his son is in jail. He speaks in an African language, then patiently explains in French to his passenger—whom we never see—that he will be unable to take him any further, owing to a family emergency. He even takes him to a taxi stand and tells him that he won't be charged, and still the presumably white Frenchman is irrationally angry and obnoxious, just as were some of the French businessmen in the opening scene with the police.

Haneke seems to be insisting on the total lack of human sensitivity that reigns in this urban environment, even to the point of irrationality, compounded by the multiple cultures and languages that lead to further confusion and irritation. Clearly, the Austrian Haneke, making his first film in France, feels no compunction about showing French people in a severely unflattering light.

The next scene introduces the quasi-Brechtian, self-reflexive theme that is one of the film's most interesting aspects, and that Haneke has spoken of as a major structuring principle against the long-take. We find ourselves in a red room and hear people talking theater talk, but we see no one. Anne then moves into the shot, looking straight into the camera, while the camera shakes a little bit, calling attention to its presence, and thus its mediating role. She approaches the camera until she is in an extreme close-up, and the dialogue, which concerns whether or not a door is locked, makes us begin to think that perhaps we are watching the making of a thriller.

The director is never seen, but suddenly a male voice, presumably his, says, "You will never get out of here," and Anne suddenly looks utterly stricken. Yet it's finally impossible to tell whether the character Anne is playing is frightened, or whether Anne herself has suddenly become genuinely afraid. When we remember that the director had offered to read the other character's lines for her to play against, however, all seems, for the moment at least, cleanly sutured. The still invisible director then says, "Show me your real face, be spontaneous, react to what's happening," and we can easily imagine this as a command coming from Michael Haneke himself, directed not toward the actress character, Anne, but toward the actress Juliette Binoche herself. This same self-conscious ambiguity will arise in later scenes as well and is related to Haneke's exploration—which was begun in *Benny's Video* and which reaches its peak in *Caché*—of the impossibility of ever fully distinguishing, at least in the context of the cinema, between reality and its representation, and thus of ever understanding the basic ontological status of any noncontextualized image. Once again, we go to black.

For the first time we meet the farmer father of Georges and Jean, but as usual we must work to establish his identity. (Haneke likes to keep his audience actively participating.) Here he eats alone while reading the newspaper in a semidarkness marked by heavy greens and blues. When Jean, Georges's brother, enters, his father offers him beets, because "that's all there is." Since Jean has told Anne that he will *never* go back to the farm, in the first scene, it's difficult to know the place this scene occupies in the story's overall chronology. Has he returned to the farm, or is it a flashback to his earlier life there? Or, for that matter, a flash-forward? Silence and alienation reign until we once again cut to black.

Our next view is a static shot of the entrance to an airplane as passengers board. Despite their obvious animation, we can't hear any of the rather lengthy exchange between the flight attendants and the ground crew; it reminds us of the deaf children at the beginning of the film, for we can *see* some form of communication taking place, but we don't have access to the code. Then we spot Maria, the Romanian woman, being taken aboard in handcuffs, in a completely de-dramatized fashion, by several policemen. By refusing to underline this narratively significant part of the action and holding it off until the very end of the scene, Haneke suddenly "narrativizes" what appears to be a long, apparently completely unmarked scene by the appearance of a character we (slightly) know. In other words, the entire scene, until this final moment, remains inscrutable because we lack the "unknown (narrative) code." In addition, a political question about globalization and multiculturalism is subtly raised concerning the irrelevance of borders in a technological age of instant displacement by jet airplane.

Then back to the "African story," with a tight shot of an emotional African woman, sobbing to some sort of witch doctor or tribal elder in a (subtitled) African language, another unknown but translated code, about her son being arrested. The camera resolutely stays on her, and Haneke refuses to give us the conventional countershot even when the man, whom we never see, is speaking. In the middle of one of his sentences—just as earlier with Georges—the image once again goes to black. With the endings of these two scenes, the idea of the fragmentary has been expanded to include speech as well. As Haneke puts it to Michel Cieutat in the interview translated for this volume, regarding "the fragmentation, I also opted for other little things like cutting during the dialogue: in the scene of the letters from the photographer, the reading is interrupted right in the middle of a word; in other sequences, a question is barely asked before the cut comes and excludes the answer. A total reality can never be seized in the cinema or in real life. We know so little!"

Next the scene shifts to Romania (we surmise), and Maria and a child are walking along a road, followed through the blowing rain by a tracking shot. Finally Maria is alone in the shot, surrounded aurally by fearsome industrial noise, and she meets a man who remains unidentified. Frankly, the segment is utterly boring, to the point that the viewer wonders whether this effect is intentional or whether the scene simply doesn't work. Is Haneke trying to convey Maria's complete lack of energy, or has the scene not in any way been narrativized, not even minimally, and thus remains completely uninvolving? The remainder of the scenes set in Romania are equally flat and unfocused and raise serious questions, never answered, about whether they have any narrative or thematic purpose beyond the obvious one of justifying Maria's later decision to return clandestinely to Paris. Judged in conventional terms, the Romanian story is clearly the weakest thread in the film.

Back to Anne, who is ironing while watching a cultural program on television about abstract painting and music. She turns down the TV and listens intently to indistinct sounds coming from another apartment. Later we learn that the sounds may have come from a child being abused, but precious little narrative information is doled out during the scene itself. After a while she puts the program back on and returns to her ironing.

After another desultory scene in Romania about Maria's family and some wedding plans, we cut to a group of deaf children vigorously playing drums, producing a powerful beat that will return at the end of the film and unite, musically at least, all the different story strands. Through the use of the drums, Haneke seems to be suggesting that the only real communication possible in a multicultural context such as contemporary urban French society is through the visceral and nonverbal. The next scene introduces us fully to Georges for the first time. Obviously just returned from Kosovo, he is going through the mail and some photographs. Eventually Anne appears, and they play another little Haneke game, pretending to be formal with one another. They are "playacting," in short, and thus recapitulating in a minor mode the scenes in which she is shown acting in her film.

The next scene seems to begin in Romania, following a truck on the road, then seamlessly becomes the French farm of Jean and Georges's father. (I freely admit that this description may be completely incorrect, as Haneke continues to serve up a maddening paucity of specific narrative information.) The father sets up a motorcycle and then disappears (though the camera holds steady for a long time on the pillar and the humanless space) until his son Jean appears and drives off on the motorcycle. Apparently this is one more fruitless gesture on the father's part to convince Jean to remain on the farm. It might be surmised that these scenes on the joyless farm are meant to represent the old France that is quickly being replaced by the new, multicultural France of the city, for better and worse. But it is also by means of this impoverished rural family that we realize that the "foreigners" marginalized in modern urban French society extend beyond the Africans and the Romanians whose lives we have also been following.

Back to Anne and Brecht. We are in an apartment in Paris, and everything seems real, but then we see a boom mic and camera moving backwards. At first the apartment seems window- and doorless, but then we move into another room with windows and we realize that we are witnessing a different scene from the same "thriller" that Anne later tells her friends that she is working on. This is followed by a wordless and chronologically indefinite scene of the farmer and Jean working and feeding the animals, before we move once again to black.

One of the film's few overtly thematic scenes follows next, in a restaurant with Anne, Georges, and two other couples having dinner. After Anne talks a little about the movie she's working on, Georges offers the opinion that life is simpler in a war zone than here. At this moment we expect that Haneke will finally begin developing an articulated thematics of the image. But no, Anne starts talking banalities about her teeth hurting. Yet it is precisely this juxtaposition of violent death and mindless dinner chatter that seems intended by Haneke to critique the sea of images that engulfs us—both those taken by Georges and perhaps those being "taken" by Haneke as well—images whose very abundance have caused them to become little more than a form of entertainment or a way to pass the time.

At this point, Amadou passes by their table and is picked up by the camera and followed, with his white girlfriend, to a table. The white waiter seems at any moment about to start making difficulties (Haneke is a master at playing with audience expectations)—but he never does. In a strange gesture, the girl takes off her watch because Amadou has indicated that he doesn't much like it, leaves it in an ashtray, and then later denies, when the waiter asks, that it's hers. For some reason she seems tense and keeps asking Amadou to return to an apparently pointless story he is telling. We switch back to the other diners, as Anne recognizes Amadou as the "troublemaker" from the movie's first scene.

In another aborted attempt to articulate a theme, their friend Françine (Arsinée Khanjian) attacks Georges for taking photographs simply to show misery because, she says, she "doesn't need it." He replies that for her it's all theory, whereas for him it's lived experience, but he agrees that he can't really articulate that feeling in his photographs themselves. "So why do you take them?" she asks, a question that Haneke is presumably also asking himself concerning the film we are watching. Alas, the issue is dropped, and Anne points out Amadou to Georges. While he is looking, the image goes to black once again.

Four more (purposely?) lackluster scenes, moving from story to story, follow. Amid a plethora of half-finished construction, Maria lies to a Romanian neighbor about having found a good job in Paris; Anne finds an anonymous note (about whose contents we are told nothing), calls Georges, and goes next door to accuse her elderly neighbor of having sent it; Amadou's mother continues to talk to the witch doctor we never see; and Jean's farmer father reads a (second) note, from Jean: "I am never coming back; please don't try to find me."

Then comes the treat of a sustained emotional scene between Anne and Georges in a supermarket. Regarding the note that she has received, Anne accuses Georges of not caring, simply washing his hands of the matter (presumably the abused child), and we wonder whether this critique is also meant to apply to his lack of emotional involvement in the photographs of various "picturesque" atrocities he has taken. After informing him that she has had an abortion, she asks, "Is there a single person you have made happy in your life?" He admits that there isn't, and though the scene ends with hugs and kisses, we sense that Anne is becoming slightly deranged, presumably from the sheer anxious tension of multicultural urban life.

We next move to a joyous, if modest, wedding party in Romania (perhaps intended to contrast with the alienated upper-middle-class urban life of Anne and Georges), then to Amadou's father castigating his middle son Demba for getting in trouble in school. Interestingly, the father speaks only in his native language, and Demba responds only in French, but they do manage to communicate nevertheless.

Multilingualism, of course, is a standard feature of the multicultural world, and it can be seen as cultural enrichment as much as a sign of fractious conflict. Here, however, it seems to principally signify the alienation that predictably occurs between generations in this new world.

Another thematic trace begins with Georges rigging up a special camera that will allow him to take photographs of anonymous passengers in the Paris métro without being seen. Again, the responsibility of the image maker is addressed, if only obliquely and ambivalently. When we see the subway photos later, we suspect that Haneke is in some way equating, beyond the fact that they have been taken by the same photographer, the previous images of faraway carnage and the sad, spiritually impoverished faces that populate the métro.

We next see Georges's father, who has, in an act of apparent desperation that harkens back to Haneke's earlier films, just killed all his animals. Is this act being offered, however tentatively, as a kind of explanation or source for Georges's inability to connect emotionally to anything? Is it something in his genes, or something related to the solitude of rural life? In any case, it's clear that the bleakness of life in the country, where everything is ostensibly more "natural" and organic, offers no viable alternative to the various urban conflicts we witness in the film.

Again to Anne as actress. She is alone on a stage, a tiny, laughing figure bathed in white light against the surrounding darkness. A reference to Malvolio accompanied by her hysterical laughter indicates that she is perhaps participating in a rather experimental performance, in French, of Shakespeare's *Twelfth Night*. She appears only as a tiny dot, and while we can hear the director whispering (one presumes it's the director—we can't see him, just as we can never see Haneke, the director of the "outer" film we are watching). A trademark Haneke moment of paranoia is evoked in Anne's plaintive question at the end of this scene: "Is someone there?"

The idea of language and its lack as unknown codes continues in the next scene, set among Amadou's relatives. The scene also contains a black, nonhearing child we see for the first time, and she inevitably reminds us of the opening sequence of the film. Multiple languages, along with sign language, contend simultaneously, while the camera refuses to budge. The girl's last question, while looking at a map, could not be more obvious in authorial intent: "Where is Africa?" she asks.

After two short scenes in which we see Georges trying out his new camera technique in the métro and people in Romania discussing the logistics of sneaking into France, we cut to a resonant scene of Georges's father François, obviously worried about Jean's disappearance, sitting at his table with Anne and Georges. He agrees that there's no future on

Figure 9. Amadou's family at table in *Code Unknown,* while his little sister signs.

the farm for Jean, and, now that he's run away, he laughs that at least Jean won't have to get up at 5:00 A.M. anymore. Anne talks about the thriller she has just been filming, called *The Collector,* while François distractedly plays with the crumbs on the table.

Next we see clandestines, including Maria, being sneaked over the European Union border, with German as the principal language heard—one more new ingredient added to the bubbling linguistic broth—and then the burial scene for "la petite Françoise," who is presumably the abused little girl that Anne had been concerned about. The camera follows Anne as she departs, in silence, with her neighbor.

Another potentially important thematic scene begins, as we see the collection of black-and-white still photos Georges has taken in the métro. Curiously enough, however, these images are accompanied by his running commentary about his adventures with the Taliban in Afghanistan, including his kidnapping. It's as though all the different sad locations are being collapsed into a single space of deprivation and otherness. Connected to this is Georges's story about one of his kidnappers, who kept asking him, in English, "What can I do for you?" until Georges finally realized that his questioner didn't actually know what the phrase meant.

Figure 10. Anne (Juliette Binoche) comforts the farmer (Josef Bierbichler) while his son Georges (Thierry Neuvic) looks on in *Code Unknown*.

Perhaps another example of an "unknown code"? An empty signifier without a signified?

In any case, the juxtaposition of the dialogue about Afghanistan with the Paris photographs seems purposeful but, as usual, unclear in intent. Georges begins to philosophize a bit, presumably continuing to argue with their friend Francine in her absence: "It's easy to talk about the ecology of images" and "the value of the nontransmitted message," he says, "but what matters is the end result. I guess she finds it all too bothersome. But after all, she could be right. How would it help her knowing [about all] that? I don't think I'm fit for life in peace. At least what you call 'peace.'"

Again, Haneke seems to want to raise various political ideas related to the nature of visual images but, never completing a thought or a theme, always forces us to pursue their implications on our own. The closest he has come to explaining this thematics is when he told Christopher Sharrett that "the film also questions whether the image transmits meaning. Everyone assumes it does. The film also questions the purpose of communication, and also what is being avoided and prevented in communication processes. The film tries to present these questions in a broad spectrum."

What follows is an almost self-consciously "beautiful" image of a tractor plowing, which may or may not be related, beyond mere proximity, to the previous scene. The frame is neatly divided between the lush green of the grass and the brown earth that has been overturned. The camera holds steady on this image as the tractor moves out of the frame, its sound becoming steadily less strong. This shot is followed by a drinking party in Romania whose joyfulness is diminished by anxious talk about having the appropriate work card. Maria, sobbing in the dark, gets to the emotional climax of her thread in the film when she speaks, with shame, of being disgusted by a Gypsy woman after giving her some money, then being despised in turn by a man who threw twenty francs at her on the Boulevard St. Germain because he found *her* disgusting.

Anne and her thriller *The Collector* follow once more, in what is probably Haneke's most effective self-reflexive scene in *Code Unknown*. Anne and an unknown man are kissing in a swimming pool in what appears to be an penthouse apartment, when suddenly we spot a child about to fall over the railing. Anne and the unknown man manage to save the child at the last moment in an impressively convincing manner, then strike him for doing something so dangerous. We find ourselves at a loss in the middle of this highly convincing and actually quite lengthy family scene. Then we cut suddenly to the two actors in a screening room *watching* the scene we have just witnessed, which they are redubbing because of an airplane that flew overhead during the take, while they begin to laugh uncontrollably.

As Haneke gleefully points out in the interview with Cieutat in this volume, "The scene in the swimming pool, for example, which was edited in the normal way [i.e., with no long-take], was taken by many people for a real scene in the film." Once again, we have been taken in by the lack of a limiting context. As Jacques Derrida has shown in *Limited, Inc.*, his famous book on J. L. Austin's speech-act theory, all meaning is dependent upon context. But since context can never be fully known or limited, meaning is always indeterminate. Haneke is showing us how this works regarding cinematic images and thus, by implication, all images. We can never be sure, in other words, of what seems so clearly evident, of what is right before our eyes. Furthermore, we understand that each time we witness a scene like this, a scene whose editing purposely clashes with that of the overall film, Haneke is contrasting the two aesthetics and thus also pointing to his own involvement in the image-making process and the audience manipulation that is its inevitable corollary.

But is there more? Does Anne's innocent, nearly hysterical laughter somehow set her—and us—up for the most powerful scene in the film, which is shortly to come?

After a brief and incomprehensible shot of cars disembarking from a ferry in an African country—we see everything through a car windshield—what comes next is clearly intended as, and magnificently works as, the emotionally climactic center of the film. We find ourselves once again in the Paris métro. Anne, as we will later discover, is sitting in the far end of the car, with her back toward us, but, in a shot that runs counter to every technique Hollywood holds dear, for the longest time we have no idea that she's there.

Two Arab teenagers enter the car at the rear, yet the camera remains at the opposite end, in its accustomed stationary long-take, and refuses to move closer for narrative clarity. However, the purposely annoying, unbalanced compositional elements contribute tellingly to the emotional and psychological power of the scene, as the viewer is carefully drawn in and played with when one of the Arab youths begins to taunt the French woman we eventually realize is Anne. As he unleashes a tirade of class and ethnic resentment on her (at one point he even mockingly refers to himself as part of the "racaille" [scum], a term that France's president, Nicholas Sarkozy, would famously use a few years later to describe troublesome Arab youth), no one in the car comes to her aid, and she finally moves to the other end, nearer to us, facing the camera.

The tension builds when the Arab youth follows Anne to the camera-end of the car and sits down beside her, continuing his abuse. Suddenly and completely unexpectedly—the shocking Haneke signature moment—he spits in her face. She is barely able to maintain her composure as an older Arab man next to her begins to defend her against his younger compatriot. Interestingly, and purposely, when they both stand, we don't see their heads as they argue, as Haneke refuses to move the camera for purposes of visual clarification, or Hollywood "professionalism," as though it were merely a neutral recording device that is trying its best to catch life in the raw. Anne, realizing that there is nothing to be done beyond enduring the experience, holds herself in emotionally and suffers in silence. Then, offscreen, the young man suddenly shouts, severely startling Anne, the older Arab man, and the entire audience. (Interestingly, it has the same effect as the suicide scene in *Caché*, and the same actor who slits his throat in the later film, Maurice Bénichou, here plays the role of the older Arab man.) Finally breaking down, Anne thanks the man, in an important gesture, and begins to sob.

It is difficult to know where the director is in all of this. Naturally, in a single iconic scene of a film, we see little of the underlying social conditions (40 percent unemployment of Arab youth, giant alienating high-rises in the Arab ghettoes of the *banlieue*, constant harassment by the police) that might cause us to side with the Arab youth in his anger. Similarly, we have been psychologically identifying with Anne (after all, she's played by Juliette Binoche!) throughout the film, and it is difficult to imagine many audience members coming away with anything but total contempt for the Arab youth. This feeling is to some extent mitigated by our respect for the older Arab man who comes to her rescue, but in going along with this ethnic stereotyping, presumably in the name of realism, Haneke is clearly playing a dangerous game. It's important to note, in other words, that his famous desire to manipulate the audience overtly can have right-wing implications as well.

The director has discussed this scene from a formal and psychological point of view, however, if not a political one, drawing a careful distinction between being manipulated and being *implicated*, that shows him at his most Brechtian:

> To create an artificial universe, one always develops a situation in which one is implicated. Which is the danger the cinema represents: you can make people believe they are implicated in a situation to the point where they're no longer capable of judging things coldly, of remaining outside. That's what most of the filmmakers who play on identification do. I, on the other hand, am always fighting a little bit against this idea of identification. I give the spectator the possibility of identifying, and immediately after, with the help of the black shots for example, I say to him or her: Stop a little bit with the emotional stuff and you'll be able to see better! (Cieutat interview in this volume)

After the usual cut to black, we come back to the powerfully stirring beat of the drums heard earlier, now being played outside, as a train goes by in the background. As we cut to Maria walking around the same area in which the film began—the location in which the precipitating incident took place that would involve all their lives—the drums continue pounding, aurally uniting the various stories as the end of the film nears. What remains visually fragmented, therefore, is at least aurally unified, and thus there is hope. As Haneke told Christopher Sharrett, "Of course the film is about [the failure of communication], but the scene of the children drumming is concerned with communication with the body, so the deaf children have hope after all, although the drumming takes on a different meaning at the conclusion when it provides a specific background."

Maria walks past the place in which the film began, past the flower shop, back and forth, with the tracking shot changing direction as needed, and finds another beggar in the spot she had earlier occupied. She stops in front of an unreadable historical sign of the sort that dot Paris, as though Haneke were underlining her absolute lack of connection with Parisian history and thus with French culture in general. With the drums still at full blast, she finally finds a suitable place to beg, but her discomfort and shame are clear. But, beyond the obvious point of an illegal immigrant's lack of a real "place" to be in this multicultural world, it is difficult to discern the director's intention here. As the drums continue, Maria is urged by area businessmen (or security guards) to take her begging elsewhere.

The drums accompany Anne out of the métro, as the camera tracks to the right, in the opposite direction from that taken by Maria, then Anne walks head-on toward the camera before it resumes its side tracking shot. She punches in the entrance code—now *connu*, at least to her—to what seems like a new apartment building. Georges arrives in a cab, in the pouring rain, and after buying her a gift in a fancy store—the drums are still pounding away—tries the code but is unable to enter. Obviously, for him, the new code remains *inconnu*. He goes to the other side of the street to shout up to the window, thinks better of it, and then goes to a payphone but apparently gets no response. He looks forlornly up at the apartment, gives up, and then hails a cab while continuing to look up, hopefully. When the image goes suddenly to black, the drums stop suddenly as well.

The final scene of the film is an obvious bookend to the first one. All three stories have now apparently "concluded." A different hearing-impaired girl (or possibly a boy) is standing alone, making those animal-like noises, as in the opening scene, that deaf people sometimes make that can upset hearing people. The child looks happy and is "talking" away, but of course we haven't a clue what he or she is saying because the code is unknown to us—Haneke provides no subtitles. Nothing is translated, and we feel what it is like to be an outsider. We see no other kids in this scene, which is much shorter than the opening scene and more immediately, if ambiguously, expressive.

For the final time we cut to black and are told that we have just watched "un film de Michael Haneke." The artist signs his work, and once again, art reigns supreme in this modernist world. When Cieutat asked the director, in the context of a discussion of *Code Unknown*, if it is true that "art is the only thing left as the last great refuge for man," the latter responded without hesitation: "Yes, I think so. Art is the only thing that can console us whatsoever! But spectators have to look for their own responses wherever they are. It's useless if they find responses that don't come from within. That can only give them a good conscience."

The Piano Teacher (2001)

The Piano Teacher, Haneke's first and only literary adaptation among his theatrically released films,[9] is quite distant in tone and theme from his earlier "glaciation trilogy" and differs significantly from his previous French-language film, *Code Unknown,* as well. Based on a 1983 novel by the difficult and often angry Austrian writer Elfriede Jelinek, who would go on to win the Nobel Prize for literature in 2004, the film generally follows the novel's plot, such as it is, as well as retaining all of the principal characters and situations. In short, looked at from one perspective, it is a remarkably faithful adaptation.

On the other hand, the novel itself is often so (purposely) irrational and bizarre, reveling in its jumbled and contradictory depiction of its characters' psychological motivation, that, owing to commercial and even dramatic and narrative exigencies, the film—and this may come as a surprise to the many who have been shocked by it—is, compared to Jelinek's novel, quite tame, formally and in terms of its subject matter.

It's clear that this is not due to any reticence or fear of offending on the part of the director. Rather, without access to the internal thoughts of the characters, which is a given in fiction, many otherwise under-standable (if strange) gestures in the novel simply could not be taken seriously if translated directly into the always external visuals of a film. Nevertheless, the film retains enough of the exotic sadomasochism of its source material to satisfy even the most jaded of art-film aficionados.

One of the apparently minor but illuminating differences between the novel and the film is that in German, the novel's title is *Die Klavier-spielerin* (The [female] piano player). In the English version, it's known as *The Piano Teacher*, which is a more accurate description of the position occupied by Erika Kohut (Isabelle Huppert), its central character. (This little change may also have indirect thematic import: in the novel, it is clearly indicated that Erika has become a teacher because she has failed as a concert pianist, but significantly, this is not mentioned in the film.)

Haneke has explained the film's title this way: "I was adapting the title of Jelinek's book, which in the original is *Die Klavierspielerin*, or 'The Piano Player,' which is a deliberately awkward title and an uncommon term in German. This is to point to Erika's degraded situation. *Pianisitin* [*sic*] is the German word for the female pianist, so the title of the novel in German is a put-down suggesting Erika's crisis. The English transla-tion of the novel is *The Piano Teacher*, which isn't correct at all, and is of course a little nonsensical and even more devaluing of the protagonist. [In the French title of the film,] I left the German title of the book not quite as it is, to give her more dignity, which is simply my approach to the material" (Sharrett).

Also, when Erika frequents the porno places in which she watches a live sex act (in the novel) or porn movies (in Haneke's film, for the obvious self-reflexive reasons that we have seen the director employ in earlier films), in the novel much is made of the fact that the men are Turks. In fact, Jelinek seems obsessed by this situation, which is not even mentioned in the film (though the visual evidence is there if one thinks to look). It is quite possible that she intends this racist attention to be a representation of what her fellow "good" Austrians would be thinking, since her views in the rest of the book are clearly at least as anti-Austrian as they could ever be construed as anti-Turk. In fact, as in most of her novels, Jelinek's view of the human race, in all its ethnic or national manifestations, is decidedly misanthropic—virtually everyone in her books is a horrible person—and Haneke, for once seeking to modulate his attack on the viewer and on bourgeois conventions, wisely soft-pedals Jelinek's obvious idiosyncrasies.

Haneke's adaptation has been called "pornographic," and his response to this attack has allowed him to make an interesting, if somewhat self-congratulatory, distinction between the pornographic and the obscene that harkens back to earlier statements about the consumability of violence and clearly links *The Piano Teacher* to his earlier work:

> I would like to be recognized for making in *La Pianiste* an obscenity, but not a pornographic film. . . . Whether concerned with sexuality or violence or another taboo issue, anything that breaks with the norm is obscene. Insofar as truth is always obscene, I hope that all of my films have at least an element of obscenity.
>
> By contrast, pornography is the opposite, in that it makes into a commodity that which is obscene, makes the unusual consumable, which is the truly scandalous aspect of porno rather than the traditional argument posed by institutions of society. It isn't the sexual aspect but the commercial aspect of porno that makes it repulsive. I think that any contemporary art practice is pornographic if it attempts to bandage the wound, so to speak, which is to say our social and psychological wound. Pornography, it seems to me, is no different from war films or propaganda films in that it tries to make the visceral, horrific, or transgressive elements of life consumable. Propaganda is far more pornographic than a home video of two people fucking. (Sharrett)

On a more formal level, Haneke's camera work in this film—including the two or three extended tracking shots that recall *Code Unknown*—is relatively straightforward, though occasionally he resorts to his earlier technique of showing only body parts, rather than faces, so that we are never sure whom we are seeing. This straightforward visual factuality also serves as a kind of cinematic equivalent of Jelinek's short, usually abrupt sentences that enforce a clinical feel throughout her story.

The other difference between the two versions is the most obvious: given her medium, many of Jelinek's effects are achieved linguistically. Her language often seems about to run off the tracks of logic and good sense, and she freely mixes the literal and the metaphoric, as for example when she describes Erika's unmotivated, surreptitious attacks on people on a bus: "SHE kicks the right heel of an old woman. SHE is able to assign every phrase its preordained location. SHE alone can take every sound and insert it in the right place, in its proper niche. SHE packs the ignorance of these bleating lambs into her own scorn, using it to punish them. Her body is one big refrigerator, where Art is well stored" (20). Elsewhere, a musical performance suddenly gets metaphorized into a page-long description of ice skating: "Gathering speed, the skater is compressed into herself by a gigantic fist: concentrated kinetic energy, hurtling out at exactly the right split second into a microscopically precise double axis, whirling around, landing right on the dot. The impact jolts her through and through, charging her with at least double her own body weight, and she forces that weight into the unyielding ice" (103). And so on. Haneke obviously doesn't have these linguistic resources at his disposal, and it's unclear what a possible cinematic "translation" of such devices might look like. Instead, what Haneke substitutes for Jelinek's scandalous language is the scandalous presence of real bodies.

Haneke's film indicates a further shift in his own work regarding character portrayal, with the characters of *Code Unknown* marking a kind of transitional point between the social and the personal. In the director's earliest theatrical films, people usually act the way they do because of the social alienation that they experience, not because of their own individual psychology. To some extent, this is still true in *Code Unknown*, though the French setting and at least one well-known actress push the film toward a greater focus on the characters' personal problems, especially that of Anne (Juliette Binoche). With *The Piano Teacher*, the shift to individual character psychology seems almost complete in the person of Erika, played brilliantly by Huppert.[10]

While the emphasis in Jelinek's novel is still to some extent on the social sources of the characters' malaise, the critic Maximilian Le Cain is right to say of the cinematic version of Erika that "while she is indubitably alienated, her angst stems not from being adrift in the depersonalised void of the modern urban environment, but from being imprisoned in a world of her own creation, governed by her own neurotic sensibility. . . . For the first time [in Haneke's films], the emotional intensity of relationships is allowed to prevail over the more detachedly analytical question of man's disconnectedness from his everyday reality." Yet Haneke has insisted that Erika is not "crazy" in any conventional sense and that his main objective is still social analysis: "'Obviously she's not mad, and that's obviously what's interesting about her. . . . In all my films, I use extremes—be they incidents or behaviour—as a way to show what is typical in our society. It is through these extreme cases that we can best depict normality'" (qtd. in Morrow).

When Christopher Sharrett asked the director if this is the film that best represents his sensibility and development, he replied, "I wouldn't say this, since the idea isn't mine but based on a novel, whereas my other films come from my own ideas. . . . Of course, I chose the topic of *La Pianiste* because I was very much drawn to it, and what I could bring to this work. But in some ways it is a bit distant from me. For example, I couldn't have written a novel on the subject of female sexuality." He put it more succinctly to Scott Foundas: "I would say that my version of looking at the story is pretty distanced and cool, while the novel itself is almost angry and very emotional. The novel is much more subjective and the film is much more objective."

Whatever its relation to its source material, Haneke's film is striking and, for the average filmgoer, one presumes, even occasionally shocking. Erika and her mother (Annie Girardot), who sleep together in the same bed at night, are locked in mortal combat, yet also emotionally codependent. Both film and book begin with a battle royale in which Erika attacks her mother physically, literally pulling out clumps of her hair, then, groveling at her feet, apologizing minutes later. In both versions, the mother must, for her own psychological reasons, control Erika at all costs, and the novel contains an occasional flashback on Erika's sexually and emotionally stunted childhood.

Haneke's accent on the conflict within this dysfunctional family is representative of a more encompassing view concerning the general psychological unhealthiness of all family life. As he told Sharrett in an uncompromising statement that deserves being quoted in full,

> I wanted first of all to describe the bourgeois setting, and to establish the family as the germinating cell for all conflicts. I always want to describe the world that I know, and for me the family is the locus of the miniature war, the first site of all warfare. The larger political-economic site is what one usually associates with warfare, but the everyday site of war in the family is as murderous in its own way, whether between parents and children or wife and husband. . . . I wanted to describe this in as

detailed a way as I can, leaving to the viewer to draw conclusions. The cinema has tended to offer closure on such topics and to send people home rather comforted and pacified. My objective is to unsettle the viewer and to take away any consolation or self-satisfaction.

One of the film's two principal emotional battlegrounds having thus been established right from the beginning, its opening credits are interspersed throughout a series of piano lessons in which the demanding Erika, under the guise of pedagogical rigor, takes obvious pleasure in humiliating several young students. The perhaps purposeful linguistic confusion that is at the heart of the film—it's a German-language novel set in Vienna, yet the film's characters speak French, though all the signage that surrounds them throughout the film is in German—is foregrounded by Haneke from the start in that what is being practiced is a German lied by Schubert, sung in German. Each time we cut to new credits, simple small white capitals against a stark black background, the music is abruptly cut off, and silence momentarily reigns.

We are soon introduced to Walter Klemmer (Benoît Magimel)—interestingly, and in a manner that presages what is to come—through the grillwork of an elevator that separates him from Erika and her mother. At least a decade younger than Erika, he will become the film's co-protagonist, or antagonist, depending on your point of view, and will shortly be engaged in intense emotional combat with the piano teacher and her mother. Haneke has made him much more educated, sophisticated, polite, and—most important—musically talented than Jelinek's Walter. In his novelistic incarnation, his physical, athletic side (represented in the film only in passing, via his membership in a hockey team) is much more heavily emphasized, especially seen against Erika's perverse but also idealized ideas about love and sex.

Haneke's changes to Walter's character actually go even further and show the director in a surprisingly accessible, even commercial, light. As he told the British critic Stuart Jeffries, "'In the novel Jelinek keeps calling Klemmer an arsehole. You can do that in a novel but in a film if you are told that a character is an arsehole, then in five seconds you see how the picture is going to end. It was important to leave Walter as an open character for possible identification'" (qtd. in Jeffries). Again, a key question for Haneke, even in the context of literary adaptation, is the manipulation of audience identification.

Similarly, the director has delineated the differences between his and Jelinek's treatments of Walter in more specific terms by saying that "the novel is written in a very cynical mode. The novel turns him from a rather childish idiot into a fascist asshole. The film tries to make him more interesting and attractive. In the film, the 'love affair,' which is not so central to the novel, is more implicated in the mother-daughter relationship. Walter only triggers the catastrophe. In the book, Walter is a rather secondary character that I thought needed development to the point that he could be a more plausible locus of the catastrophe" (Sharrett). These somewhat self-contradictory comments clearly show that Haneke's relationship to Jelinek is at best a quasi-adversarial one. It should also be noted that for whatever strategic or polemical reasons of his own, Haneke inaccurately describes Walter's status in the novel as "a rather secondary character."

At their first meeting, Erika and Walter discuss Schumann and Schubert, and Erika asks whether Walter has read Adorno on Schumann's "Fantasia in C Major," an essay that concerns Schumann's music just before he fell into madness.[11] Haneke also uses a technique that we have seen in his earlier films, especially in *Code Unknown,* of keeping the camera resolutely on Erika, even though they are having a two-way conversation, with not a single shot/reverse shot to mitigate the visual intensity of focusing solely on her face, which remains utterly expressionless. Reaction shots are infrequent here and in the other later Haneke films, perhaps as another way to distinguish his work from standard-issue Hollywood fare.

Another Hanekean technique that reappears is one that was used to particular advantage in *Benny's Video*: the extended sound bridge, especially moving from a scene of banality or vulgarity to a scene in which classical music is being played or sung, with obvious thematic implications. Haneke uses this technique to move into and out of Erika's first visit to the porn place, strangely (for Americans, at least) located in some sort of shopping mall.

Once she enters the mall, Erika is followed by Haneke's familiar tracking shot and finally settles into her private cabin to watch a lively scene of fellatio on video. Apparently desirous of involving her other senses as well in her erotic pleasure, she plucks a used tissue from an adjacent waste basket to sniff while watching. This is followed by a long audio bridge of a male voice singing a lied in German, which is especially noteworthy juxtaposed with the moans and groans emanating from the porn video. One can hardly imagine a better representation of the contrast between the flesh and the spirit, between commercialized, "consumable" sex, with its attendant bodily fluids, and sanitized high culture. Interestingly, even more seems at stake in the novel, in which Jelinek's narrator discusses the relation between porn films and other films. Her narrator chillingly concludes that "in its supreme form, pain is a variety of pleasure. Erika would gladly cross the border to her own murder" (107). Matters are quite a bit less extreme in Haneke's film, however—it seems strange to think of him as the conservative one—and besides, Jelinek's narrator's remark may merely represent an aspect of Erika's fantasy life, not a conscious wish.

Erika is up to more than just porno watching and semen sniffing, however, and soon enough we are alone with her in the bathroom as she sets about, in her characteristic workmanlike manner, to slash her genitals with a razorblade. An apparently intentional whiff of black humor is added when we hear her mother, offscreen, calling her to dinner, while her blood courses down the side of the bathtub. "Coming, mother!" she chirpily replies, causing the audience to giggle. A few minutes later, Erika's mother spots blood running down her leg, assumes that it's menstrual blood, and points out how disgusting it is.

A more lighthearted component, relatively speaking, of Erika's sadomasochism comes out when she finds one of her young male students in a store perusing porn magazines with his friends. Later, during his piano lesson, she continues to torment him about it in an ice-cold manner, despite his apologies, suggesting that he bring his mother along with him the next time.

In the meantime, the already highly accomplished Walter Klemmer is accepted by the conservatory as her student, despite Erika's unconvincing, halfhearted objections to his admission to the program. Soon enough, he confesses his love for her and again; owing to the necessary simplifications inherent to the cinematic form, it all seems to be little more than a matter of the standard crush students sometimes develop toward teachers whose intellect and abilities they respect, rather than the contradictory, even dangerous feelings that swirl between these two figures in Jelinek's version.

Though Haneke has claimed that he has made Walter a more important character than he is in the novel, he has clearly decided to focus on the scandalous sadomasochism of Erika rather than repeating Jelinek's obvious loathing of Walter's animal vitality and self-assurance—in other words, his sheer maleness ("She thinks he is referring to Schubert, but he really means himself, just as he always means himself whenever he speaks" [120]). In the film he comes off as a bit aggressive, certainly, but also polished and even, at times, rather dashing. Despite rebuffing his advances, Erika is clearly intrigued and follows him to his hockey practice, which she watches from afar.

Her next transgressive act is to prowl a drive-in movie theater (rather than the empty field of Vienna's famous Prater amusement park, as in the novel), looking for couples engaged in sex. This is an absolutely appropriate substitution for the image-obsessed Haneke to make, especially since it is accompanied by his trademark tracking shot. The cinematic images of the drive-in are particularly impressive because they loom gigantically, out of focus, behind her and seem to be making a silent comment on the deleterious ubiquity of such artificially generated, easily consumable images in our culture. After all, if many young people go to the drive-in to have sex in the presence of these overwhelming images, how different is the functioning of the porn video shop she has earlier visited? (As Jacques Lacan might point out, the image is now gazing at the spectator—as it always has been.) After finding a couple making love, she looks in the car window and, while listening to their moaning, decides to urinate between the cars. (In the movie it is implied that this is her rather offbeat response to her own sexual stimulation, whereas the book makes it clear on several occasions that her urination is involuntary, something that, in these situations, she can't control.) When she is spotted by the young man in the car, he takes off after her, but she escapes.

Another display of an overtly sadistic act arises from the jealousy Erika experiences when Walter shows kindness to a promising female student whom Erika has, perversely, been particularly mean to, despite the student's talent and devotion to her. The student, who is to accompany the male lieder singer in a concert, is so upset by Erika's criticism that her diarrhea keeps her from performing, but Walter cheers her up enough to enable her to go on stage. Haneke keeps the camera fixed on Erika's expressionless face for the longest time, as she listens to the music the girl is playing while considering what action to take. Finally she decides to break up a glass and put the dangerous pieces in the coat pocket of her perceived rival for Walter's attention. When, at the end of the concert, the girl's scream is heard offscreen (in an efficient Hitchcockian moment), Erika plays the innocent with complete aplomb.

Owing to her urinary compulsion at moments of stress (as explained in the novel), she heads to a bathroom (which is spare and antiseptic in the film, disgustingly filthy in the novel), followed by Walter, who tries to overwhelm her with passionate kisses, to which she only partially responds. Clearly, she wants to humiliate him by controlling every aspect of the sexual situation, though some will perhaps see her actions as reclaiming a balance of power in a relationship that, under patriarchy, is always by definition unequal. Thus, she pulls his zipper down and masturbates him, but she won't let him kiss her and tells him that if he moves even slightly, she will leave. As one of my students pointed out, this is a kind

Figure 11. The first sexual encounter of Erika (Isabelle Huppert) and Walter (Benoît Magimel), in the music conservatory men's room, in *The Piano Teacher*.

of (at least symbolic) rape of Walter that parallels the real one that he will inflict on Erika later in the film.

Walter, obviously none too happy about having lost all power in the situation, also complains that she is hurting him. She kneels for fellatio, but all that we witness, from his waist up, are his contradictory reactions of pleasure and unease. She tells him that she will give him a letter in which all of her "instructions" will be made clear and then refuses to finish masturbating him. Nor will she let him continue on his own—though she insists that he keep his penis out while facing her—and then finally goes back to coldly masturbating him again. By the end of this bizarre sexual encounter, Walter laughs, playfully smacks her and, demonstrating that this normal young man hasn't a clue as to what has just happened, promises that their lovemaking "will go better next time."

At their next (musical) practice session, Erika gives Walter the letter of sexual instruction, while he continues to entertain the illusion that she is interested in a conventional love affair and begs to kiss her neck. When he asks her to "loosen up," she replies, "I have no emotions, Walter, and if I do, they will never defeat my intelligence."

Later that night (or, possibly, another night), Walter accosts Erika in the hallway of her apartment building. She dismisses him, but he won't go away, and Erika allows him, despite her mother's strong objections, to enter their apartment. Erika insists he read the letter, full of its precise directions as to how he is to beat, humiliate, and lock her up, while her mother frets in front of the television in the next room, afraid that she is going to lose her dominance over Erika.

Repelled by her requests, Walter nevertheless tries to initiate the conventional lovemaking that he is familiar with and unreasonably continues to expect, while she demonstrates the sadomasochistic sex equipment that she has collected for their use. "Do I disgust you?" she asks. "The urge to be beaten has been in me for years. From now on, it's you who gives the orders. You will choose what I will wear." This neat reversal is Haneke's tidy dramaturgical way of translating Jelinek's internally expressed realization that Erika's method of maintaining complete control is by *insisting* that she be reduced to utter powerlessness. ("Did he get it right: By becoming her master, he can never become her master? So long as she dictates what he should do to her, some final remnant of Erika will remain unfathomable" [Jelinek 216].)

Walter's response to Erika can only be that of the bourgeois he is: "You are sick. You need treatment." "Hit me if you want," she pleads. "I wouldn't touch someone like you even with gloves," he replies. "Right now you repulse me, though I loved you."

Once Walter has left, Erika, presumably aroused after she has retired to bed with her mother, begins kissing her wildly while sobbing like a wounded animal. Recoiling, her mother tells her that she is completely crazy. "I saw your pubic hair," Erika informs her by way of response, a line that clearly represents Haneke's bid to vie, at least occasionally, with Jelinek (who speaks of the same thing in this scene, though as part of the narrator's third-person internal discourse rather than in the spoken dialogue) in pursuing the sexually transgressive.

In a scene set in the equipment room of Walter's hockey team, a scene added by Haneke that nicely parallels their first sexual encounter in the bathroom, Erika takes a completely different tack. Apologizing for the shock of the letter, she says that she now realizes that they should have talked it over first. Begging his forgiveness, desperately pledging her love for him (presumably the "normal" kind of love that he has been

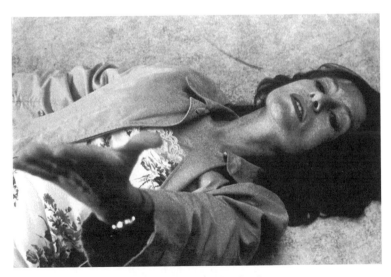

Figure 12. Erika (Isabelle Huppert) pleads
with Walter (Benoît Magimel) for sex
in his locker room in *The Piano Teacher*.

seeking), she wildly digs at his pants in search of his penis, while the ever-conventional Walter worries about being discovered.

He is still fully dressed in his massively padded hockey uniform, and this fact plus the expressive mise-en-scène—a plethora of hockey equipment that surrounds them—bizarrely and brilliantly adds to the incongruousness and power of the scene. Given the arrangement of the thrusting bodies, Walter seems to be plunging his penis into her mouth, though it can't be clearly seen. Her response is to throw up violently (the novel speaks of her "gorge rising"). Stung by what he takes as yet another rejection of his offer of "normal" sex, Walter launches into a tirade about how disgusting she smells, as she becomes more and more abased. "You need to wash your mouth more often, not just when my cock makes you sick," he tells her. Is she genuinely humiliated, against her will, or, given the proclivities she has expressed orally and in the letter, is this humiliation precisely what she seeks from him? This will become, in a certain sense, the central question of the entire film.

In the penultimate scene of the film (at this point Haneke, probably wisely, omits two scenes from the novel, one in which Erika puts clothespins and sharp pins on and into her skin and another—which parallels Erika's earlier nighttime foray into the Prater—in which Walter goes looking for an animal to kill in order to express his frustration), Erika is in bed with her mother when Walter begins impatiently ringing the doorbell.

Once inside the apartment, he informs Erika that he was masturbating under her window and expresses his humiliation at having been reduced to that. Unfortunately, this is another example of a moment in which the movie, by following the book, demonstrates its courage and power but also comes off, especially in terms of character motivation, as inexplicable and illogical, because we aren't privy to Jelinek's complicated (and often contradictory) verbal descriptions of the characters' mental processes.

Still obviously upset by the contents of Erika's letter, Walter locks up her mother in the bedroom and begins smacking Erika around, ultimately breaking her nose. Justifying his actions, he angrily quotes from the letter of "instructions," but now she pleads for him *not* to hit her, claiming that she was completely wrong and that she has now changed her mind about what she wants from him. But is she being honest here—whatever being "honest" might mean—or is this an indirect way of manipulating the angry Walter to pleasure her by beating her up? Is she powerless at

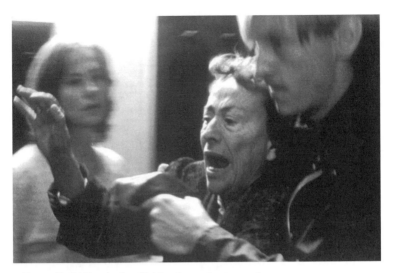

Figure 13. Walter deals with his other adversary, Erika's mother (Annie Girardot), as Erika (Isabelle Huppert) looks on in *The Piano Teacher*.

this point, or all-powerful? When her breast is revealed, he says, "Don't show me your disgusting body."

Walter gets Erika to admit that she is "partly responsible" for what is happening, because "you can't get a guy all excited then put him on ice. We can't just play by your rules. You can't delve around inside people then reject them." At first feigning affection, or perhaps feeling it after his own fashion, Walter soon turns toward rape as the quickest way to make himself feel better. She begs him to stop, while he simply demands that she love him and continues to thrust away as she remains limp. At this point, audience sympathy, presumably, is fully against Walter. But could it not also be the case that Erika's convincing expression of her fear of being hurt is accomplishing exactly what she really desires? After he's finished, he warns her not to tell anyone, since it's for her own good anyway: "You can't just humiliate a guy." Oh, and, "Will you be all right?" he gently asks, bewilderingly reversing course. "Do you need anything? You know, love isn't everything."

In the final scene, the next morning, Erika picks up a knife from the kitchen as she and her mother get ready to go to the concert in which Erika will substitute for the girl whose hand she is responsible for cruelly maiming. At the conservatory, Erika seems to be looking for Walter, who finally bounces up, in supremely happy fashion, with a group of friends. Now alone, Erika cries softly and suddenly stabs herself in the shoulder, causing a wound whose blood spreads across her light-colored blouse. (In the novel, Jelinek mentions several times that Erika has no idea whether she is going to stab Walter [significantly, in front of the engineering school, where he began his studies, rather than at the conservatory] or not, right up until the last minute.)

In the eyes of this viewer, at least—though obviously other readings may be equally plausible—this act of self-mutilation provides a retroactive explanation of what has occurred the previous night. She is, in fact, still in thrall to her masochistic desires—perhaps in order to escape the emotional domination of her mother that has stunted her life—and thus it makes sense to read Walter's assault and rape as intentionally induced by Erika and as producing exactly the effect she was aiming for. (In at least one interview, Haneke refuses to say whether Erika "gets what she wants at the end of the film," though several commentators have simply assumed that she has been sexually violated against her will.)

The second-to-last shot of the film foregrounds the symmetry of two different sets of doors leading to the interior concert space, as though to reestablish a kind of classical order akin to that of classical music—say, that of Haydn or Mozart—above the irrational level of human passion. Then the very last shot does the same thing, but now outside, as the cars whiz by the beautifully lighted entrance and grillwork, their drivers and passengers unconscious of the "illicit," irrational human desires that have just been enacted inside. As always, it's purposely unclear, but Haneke seems to be saying that Erika has come full-circle and has achieved at least part of what she has been searching for all along.

So what does it all add up to? As Sharrett directly asked the director, are "sexual relationships . . . impossible under the assumptions of the current society?" "We are all damaged," replied Haneke, "but not every relationship is played out in the extreme scenario of Erika and Walter. Not everyone is as neurotic as Erika. It's a common truth that we are not a society of happy people, and this is a reality I describe, but I would not say that sexual health is impossible." On the basis of the evidence provided by *The Piano Teacher*, however, Haneke's sentiment seems more wishful thinking than reality.

Time of the Wolf (2003)

Time of the Wolf (Le Temps du loup), like Haneke's two previous films, is in French (for the most part) and presumably, like *Code Unknown,* set in France, though neither the name of that country nor the name of "the city" (as it's occasionally referred to) is ever mentioned in the film. Conceived some years earlier than *The Piano Teacher*, the success of the latter film finally allowed Haneke to obtain funding to make it.

Its plot is basic, nearly nonexistent: Adrift among strangers, a family comprised of a mother named, as usual, Anne (Isabelle Huppert), and her two children, Eva and Benny, struggles to survive after an apparently apocalyptic but never-explained "event." With the elimination of all back story and the intentional vagueness of its conflicts—or rather their reduction to one simple and all-consuming conflict, survival—the film remains, intentionally or not, emotionally abstract and largely uninvolving.

To my mind, the basic difficulty with the film, which remains nevertheless quite interesting in formal terms, is encapsulated in Haneke's remarks in the interview included on the DVD: "I didn't want to make another disaster film, but a very personal film about interhuman behavior. Especially if now you turn on the TV, in every newscast you see a little bit of the end of the world. But it's always far away, affecting other people. And I wanted to do a film for our superfluous society, which feels good and comfortable, which is watching the end of the world on TV because it's far away. And to give a taste of what it would feel like if it happened to you." Guided by this quotation, it is possible to say that *Time of the Wolf* is a good if negative example of what happens when a director's ongoing, obsessive desire to condemn a society, especially in terms of its representation in the media, overrides all other considerations.

Visually, it is a return of sorts to the rigorous formal abstraction of the earlier films, unlike, say, *Code Unknown*, whose frame is generally jammed with "stuff," but stuff that is arranged in no particular logical spatial order. Yet precisely because of its atmosphere of never-specified crisis and its back-to-basics survival mode, the film also avoids a representation of the plethora of manufactured objects that oppressed the characters, and us, in the films of the "glaciation trilogy." It is precisely its chilling depiction of a world empty of these objects that gives *Time of the Wolf* the quiet power it indubitably contains.

Lighting contributes heavily to this sense of minimalist abstraction. From beginning to end, chiaroscuro rules, as though Haneke had the painters Caravaggio or, better perhaps, Georges de la Tour, in mind when he designed the look of the film. Virtually every scene is cast either in almost total darkness (often illuminated by a painterly single-light source, like the shrouded candles employed by de la Tour) or in full, if not blinding, light.

One effect of this visual dichotomy is to formally embody the black-and-white themes of good and evil that structure the film intellectually. This stark binary is visually embodied in the standard Haneke film credits, which are cast as simple, small white letters against a black background, with no music or other sound to mitigate the intensity of the visual abstraction thrust before us. The title is itself expressive. Indeed, the time in which our characters are living is not the time of "humanity" but the time of the wolf, when danger lurks everywhere and humans have been reduced to a brute animal existence.

The opening scene of the film is strongly reminiscent of the opening of *Funny Games*, with a bourgeois, nuclear family, in their van, moving quietly through the countryside (here represented by a close-up of tree trunks, which will become a frequent visual motif in the film) and then pulling up in front of their vacation place. Once they enter, they are accosted by a semicrazed man with a gun, intent on protecting his own family, apparently driven to madness by some disaster that has occurred but about which we learn nothing. As in *Funny Games*, the just-arrived, middle-class, eminently *reasonable* father tries to negotiate logically with the interlopers—in the process, he even invokes the sacred bourgeois principle of private property—but this time around he is almost immediately killed.

This nuclear family doesn't seem to have the slightest idea concerning the reason for the sudden violence, yet Anne's relatively subdued response hints that maybe they do understand and that the unnamed, even unmentioned "event" is the reason they have left "the city" for their vacation home in the first place. (The ever-reticent Haneke gives us no narrative help here.) Dad is shot point-blank, but, as usual, we don't actually see him shot; rather, we cut quickly away to several different reaction shots of the children outside—if such utterly blank faces can be said to be "reacting"—followed by a close-up of Anne, as we hear the murderer's wife screaming on the sound track. Anne, casually or in a state of shock, wipes her face of the blood that has splashed from her husband's wound, then vomits.

The next shot, the first of many perfectly framed, purposely over-aestheticized picture-book images, is an extreme long shot that is bisected horizontally, with the road in the middle, green grass in the front, lower half, and the trees and blue sky occupying the upper half. These aggressively beautiful, artificially composed, and frequently repeated images seem to represent the perfection that resides in a purely aesthetic world, one that is so far from the reality that exists just below the thin veneer of human civilization in this "time of the wolf" and thus, by extension, during all times and places. (Or are these images an expression of uncorrupted nature—the opposite pole of another binary opposition that has nothing to do with the self-destructive activities of human beings?) A distant, unrecognizable figure, probably Anne, moves along the road.

Anne seeks help from others and, as in many Haneke films, is repeatedly turned down. The director seems to be suggesting that when human beings are reduced to survival mode, little of the "human" remains. (The animal world, represented by Benny's green canary and the horses that are shot for meat, comes in for even more punishment and bewilderment. In other scenes, their maggot-ridden bodies are strewn about the landscape.)

Much of what immediately follows takes place in areas of total darkness that are occasionally punctuated by strong lighting from huge blazes. These immense fires carry their own symbolic freight of apocalypse, destruction, and damnation, as well as a kind of "visual violence" that subtly affects the viewer. These vivid contrasts are replicated on the aural track as well, where a complete lack of dialogue, along with diminished sound effects, alternates with moments of violent, anonymous screaming.

Sometimes the particularly picturesque visuals feature a gray, foggy atmosphere, a kind of luminal visibility that mitigates the binary quality that otherwise predominates. In several highly aestheticized shots, instead of the normally bright, sunny day (which itself is in ironic counterpoint to the situation that the humans find themselves in and attests once again to the indifference of nature to human suffering), what we see instead through a miasmic fog is, apparently, a series of farm buildings. We cut among different structures, but all remains indistinct. This particular series of shots is followed by an extreme long shot, from the end of a deserted road, in which we see the three members of the family struggling along their journey to nowhere. What is emphasized once again is their isolation yet at the same time, like the famous shot in the fog in Antonioni's *Red Desert* (1964), the indistinctness of borders of any kind, including the one between self and other, or self and nonself.

Despite the brusque brutality shown by most of the people that Anne and her children encounter in their wandering, some are more caring. Mr. Azoulay, the most humane and sensitive character of all, is played by the Arab-French actor Maurice Bénichou, who had a small but crucial role in *Code Unknown* as the older Arab man who defends Anne on the métro and who plays an even more salient part in *Caché*.

In addition to the kindness that emanates from a character like Mr. Azoulay, however, in this film Haneke seems to show a greater respect for family bonds than in any of his other films. Looked at negatively, this might signify that in survival mode, your family is the only thing you can count on, but Anne shows a consistent, powerful concern for her children that seems to be positively affirmed and that belies Haneke's negative comments about the family as the embodiment if not the source of all human conflict that was quoted in the previous section.

In fact, her entire motivation or "character psychology" throughout the film seems to stem from her desire to protect her family. Perhaps the most powerful expression of this atavistic familial bond comes in the scene in which Benny disappears, a sequence that begins with a gorgeous, painterly shot through a window, illuminated by the luscious dark blue light that proliferated in Haneke's early films. The mother and daughter are desperate to keep the fire going, with the aid of a failing cigarette lighter, because otherwise they will never again find Benny nor each other in the total darkness. Even this emotionally wrought, frantic moment is counterpointed with the beautiful illumination emanating from the fire, which creates red and gold highlight effects. "Eva, je t'aime," says Anne, feelingly.

It is at this moment, perhaps, that Haneke's core theme of "humanism," as he would put it, is expressed. As he says in the DVD interview, "I try in all my films to be a 'humanist' because I think if one is seriously interested in art, you can't do it any other way. Humanism is the sine qua non. Art cannot exist without humanism; it would be a contradiction. It's the most important reason for working. Communication is also a humanistic act. Refusing to communicate is a terrorist act that provokes violence." Thus, all of Haneke's themes and obsessions—humanity, communication (and its lack), art, violence—come together in one simple equation.

After a cut to extreme darkness once again, as Anne hopefully asks the shadows, "Is someone there?" another sudden cut takes us to the site of a raging inferno, as Eva has carelessly allowed the barn to catch fire. Though they argue about whose fault it is, and both are emotionally upset, Anne, ever the conscientious mother, tries to succor her daughter and not to blame her for the mishap.

Benny is returned by a wild child who suddenly materializes after the barn has burned down. The Hanekean night blue prevails once again, and the unknown, unkempt boy asks what the family will give him in return if he gives them some of his precious water. Money is now worthless in this perforce barter economy. The next day, while Anne is treating the dog bite on the newcomer's hand, he speaks of a train station where one can bribe the personnel to be permitted entry. Thenceforth this station becomes their goal and, once they reach it, the locus of the rest

Figure 14. The Wild Child (Hakim Taleb) is tended to by Anne (Isabelle Huppert) in *Time of the Wolf*.

of the film. At least one extreme long shot of the train tracks stretching into the distance is isolating—and thus alienating—and also beautiful, a tension the director works throughout. When a train does pass them, they chase after it, but to no avail.

Once they reach the station, the multicultural, multilingual dynamics of *Code Unknown*, along with the attendant conflict, prevail. Some of the station's inhabitants speak in Eastern European languages and/or broken French, others in native or lightly accented but fluent French. The chiaroscuro lighting effects return in this interior that also has an exterior, to which its denizens frequently repair, continuing the binary logic of the film. It is clear that the rules for civilized life and the maintenance of one's humanity will be under great stress in this unaccustomed situation.

A mystical or mythical element appears when the friendly Béa (Brigitte Rouan, a film director in her own right) explains to Anne the existence of "the Just," a group fixed at thirty-six members who "assure that God will protect us." Béa's question is whether the tough-guy camp organizer Koslowski (Olivier Gourmet, a Belgian actor who appears often in the films of the Dardennes brothers) is a member of that group. Later in the film, another man babbles about the Just and "the sacrifices they make for us. Their job is to keep the old ball spinning? But when there are fewer than thirty-six, everything is thrown out of whack. Let's make another group." "The real champions of world redemption," he concludes, "are my Brothers of Fire." Though neither mythic group is mentioned again in the course of the film, here they seem to be invoked to demonstrate how humans naturally turn toward myth and the propitiation of a constructed divinity, in severely difficult times, to understand what is happening to them and how to remedy their situation.

Arguments ensue concerning the best course of action, in a desultory, vague fashion that faintly resembles the debates between Estragon and Vladimir in Samuel Beckett's *Waiting for Godot*. On his portable radio, Azoulay hears vague news reports about "the situation," while Lise Brandt (Béatrice Dalle) suddenly starts screaming at a woman who has been praying obsessively since her husband was hit by a train. Finally, Lise's husband Thomas (Patrice Chéreau) slaps Lise, and she apologizes. (The fact that Chéreau is also a film director, like Brigitte Rouan, may be simply an accident of casting or Haneke's tongue-in-cheek attempt at self-reflexivity.) Anne breaks down and appeals to them to stop their bickering for the sake of the children.

A major subplot in the film now begins to unfold, concerning the relation of Eva and the "wild child" (Hakim Taleb), who is never named. He tells her about having to kill his dog after the dog bit him. Eva tries to care for the young boy, but their tentative attempts at intimacy and communication are crushed by the cruel environment into which they've been thrust, a theme, in its most general outlines, that has preoccupied Haneke since the beginning of his career. All that Eva gets in return is a "whatever you want" when she is looking for a "thank you," but the wild child does finally give her a pair of glasses in exchange for taking care of him. We later witness the barter system in its most basic form when a woman inside the station, speaking a foreign language, begs for water in exchange for sex.

Haneke next employs an interesting narrative technique that carries its own unique emotional resonance. Eva begins writing a letter to her dead father, which provides a useful summary overview of all that happens in the makeshift camp—without having to take the trouble to dramatize it—as well as an index to the inner psychological state of at least one character. (A similar technique is used in *The Seventh Continent*, in the letters to the grandparents.) In the course of narrating this letter in voiceover, Eva narrates the story of the film as well. Thus she reports on the state of the family, providing a day-to-day summary of their lives, and informs her dead father, and us, that she "writes to understand it all herself." Simultaneously we see unconnected scenes of destruction that remind us of the strong images that mark the "glaciation trilogy." Her voice suddenly stops, and we get a picture of the forest (continuing the motif of the strongly foregrounded individual trees, perhaps a signifier for the confusion that reigns), including the work detail that she is, in a way, silently explaining in voiceover. In a sense, what happens next is produced narratively from her letter.

We (barely) see someone sobbing in the dark, babbling in a language that is not translated by subtitles. It's typical and thematically important for Haneke to allot so much time to this kind of incomprehensibility. The voices and cries themselves, though empty of meaningful content, are expressive in their own right—and thus they *communicate* almost like a strange song or chant, or like the drums played by the deaf people at the end of *Code Unknown*. Tiny lights appear in the upper right-hand corner of the frame, as the unintelligible voice dies out.

Extending the system of strong contrasts on which the film is built, next comes a sudden cut to the bustling activity of a group of determined men carrying things onto the abandoned train car that occupies the track, while fires burn all around. A system by which men and women take baths at different times is established, demonstrating that the incipient anarchy has not yet manifested itself and that a thin layer of civilization still holds. The men plan, surreptitiously, to kill the water sellers' horses the next day, for dinner.

Fights inevitably break out, and often, as in many internecine conflicts, they are based on things that have happened earlier and elsewhere. Thus the "Polacks" are attacked, first verbally, then physically, by a man obviously carrying a specific grudge from a previous encounter. (Similar scenes return several times later in the film.) Haneke's wandering camera keeps returning to an old man who can't speak French, who gives his wife something to drink while Anne watches. Then Eva and Anne hear the unmistakable strains of classical music, a rather obvious signifier, it must be admitted, of the threatened but defiantly inextinguishable voice of "civilization" that Haneke has had recourse to in earlier films. (One is grateful that it is not the opening bars of Beethoven's Fifth Symphony or Pachelbel's "Canon in D Major"; the director is too sophisticated for that.) Later Eva questions the young man, who rewinds the audio tape with his finger to save the dying battery, about the music.

When daytime comes, we are once again treated to a beautifully photographed extreme long shot, this time of a green and white building in the middle of a perfectly bisected image, green grass in front, blue sky on top, that bears an exact structural relation, in its embodiment of perfection and abstraction, to earlier still shots that were primarily of natural objects. The grass blows, gorgeously, in the wind. These shots seem to represent a kind of ideal, classical stasis (like the final shots of the classical building in *The Piano Teacher*) that has been lost in the current mode of survival and a precarious civilization. Significantly, they rarely include human beings. Inside, people go about their everyday business, as during every other natural or manmade disaster: a woman suckles an infant, a man shaves, and another man reattaches his false leg.

Suddenly, a screaming match (another instance of Haneke's use of quick and unexpected change in dynamic range) breaks out between Anne and the man who has killed her husband, or at least who she thinks has killed him. An apparently self-appointed leader tells Anne that he can't do anything in the absence of proof. While they argue, we see the horses slaughtered for their meat in an extremely graphic manner, as though to make manifest the potential violence that is coagulating, just below the surface, within the humans. Rain follows, looking a little like blood, as the horses run aimlessly to and fro. Eva desperately looks for her little brother, and once she finds him shivering under a train car, she protects him with a cover and hugs him. Obviously, at least on a familial level, the best and most "humanistic" impulses have yet to be eliminated. Later, Eva and Anne embrace as well.

It turns out that the nameless wild child was actually responsible for stealing a goat, a theft attributed to the "Polack," a misattribution that almost gets the man killed, and Eva upbraids the child for not coming forward. In a psychological breakthrough, a victory for values and civility, the child actually says he is sorry. We then learn that another girl, the daughter of M. Azoulay, has committed suicide, and after a powerful shot of her naked body being washed for burial (a sight witnessed by Benny), her bereaved father distributes her clothes. We cut to the close shot of the dense tree trunks for the third or fourth time, and we watch as the wild child has to kill the goat to keep it from bleating, thus revealing his hiding place to the men who are looking for him and the goat. Eva, now disgusted by her potential companion, says, "I thought you could help me, but you ruin everything."

Night falls again, continuing an alternating rhythmic and elemental pattern of day and night, dark and light, that structures the entire film. In a scene with powerful ritualistic overtones, among the most visually striking images in the film, we see Benny walking toward a fire, his mouth smeared with blood, almost as though in a trance. He stares at this fire that burns on the track, then throws brush on it to make it burn brighter. In a strongly composed image, he stands at the far left of the frame, while the fire blazes on the right.

Perhaps in emulation of the burial rites for the young suicide that he has just witnessed, he takes off his jacket. After a cut to a very dark shot, then an extreme long shot of the fire, we see Benny standing in front of it as he begins to take all of his clothes off, apparently readying himself to jump into the flames. A unknown man shouts at him and begins to approach, but the skittish boy moves closer and closer to the flames. Finally, the man tricks Benny into looking away and is able to grab him in time to prevent another suicide.

He asks Benny where his parents are, as the camera pulls slowly back into an extreme long shot that rivals the aesthetic and emotional power of anything we have seen thus far. "You were ready to do it, that's enough," he tells Benny comfortingly. "Maybe tomorrow a big car will come and a guy will get out and say everything will be all right and we'll eat roasted pigeon and maybe the dead will come back to life." By this point, the camera has pulled back and up, from which position it seems to assume an almost godlike perspective. "It's enough that you were ready to do it. Don't worry. I'll tell everybody about it," the man assures Benny, apparently convinced that what is principally at stake for Benny is some species of male honor. Since the scene is so heavily foregrounded, yet the thoughts seem so alien to Haneke's worldview, it's difficult to know where the director stands at this climactic moment of the film.

A sudden cut takes us inside a speedily moving train on a bright and beautiful day, from which we see the lovely green countryside. We have

Figure 15. Benny (Lucas Biscombe) approaches the apocalyptic fire in *Time of the Wolf*.

no idea who is running the train or where it is going. And whose point of view is being represented here? It is impossible to say, as there are no reverse shots that would reveal the source of the gaze. It's another instance of the signature Haneke tracking shot, now moving more quickly than ever but not following anything human or even animal, for that matter. It's as though the humans have all been saved and are elsewhere, or they have all been wiped out. As far as nature is concerned—the nature we have seen throughout the film in those perfect, impossible shots—it's all the same. The only sound we hear is the rhythmic clicking of the train on the tracks. There is a sudden cut to black, and the film ends.

Caché (2005)

Caché begins with what has quickly become known as one of the most striking openings in cinematic history. An unexceptional, rigorously stationary shot of a nondescript house in Paris, partially hidden by the usual, ubiquitous string of parked cars, holds for what seems an unconscionably long time. Most importantly, and most annoyingly (or fascinatingly) for the audience, the shot seems completely unmotivated. Who is looking and why?

The first thing that alters the image is a highly imaginative credit sequence that lists all we need to know, including the film's title and entire cast and crew, in an innovative, additive (rather than substitutive) presentation of information, all of which remains onscreen throughout the sequence. Since everything is added and nothing removed, the effect is to accentuate even further the stationary quality of the single, nonmoving image that provides the background for the credits. When the credits finally disappear, the camera nevertheless remains utterly still. Our earlier and continuing makeshift assumption that it's simply a shot offered from the point of view of the director's camera begins to seem doubtful.

We hear only ambient, natural sounds, like the chirping of birds. A young woman, perhaps Anne Laurent (Juliette Binoche, playing yet another Anne), leaves the house, and a few seconds later a man whizzes by on a bicycle. The static shot that remains is primarily composed of strong vertical and horizontal lines, with little that is round or amorphous in shape. Suddenly we hear unattributed voices talking about the image.

"Well?" a man's voice says. "Nothing," replies a woman. "Where was it?" he asks. "In a plastic bag in the door," is the reply. The result of this exchange is a radical but unintelligible division between the apparently stuck image that we can't seem to get rid of and these unidentified voices whose bodies we can't see.

The woman asks, "What's wrong?" We cut to a closer shot of cars and finally see those who will become the principal protagonists, Georges Laurent (Daniel Auteuil, playing one more Georges) and Anne Laurent, emerging from the house and walking between the parked cars. It's from a different, closer angle and is presumably a "live" shot from the point of view of the filmmakers, or rather the film called *Caché*, as opposed to the videotape *within* the film that Georges and Anne, and we, have been watching. But we can never be sure, and the definitive source or context of any given represented visual field, as with *Benny's Video, Funny Games,* and *Code Unknown,* will be forever occluded. How can we tell the difference between the "intentional" Haneke footage (the film *Caché*) and the videotape footage produced within the diegesis of that film, especially since both are shot with a big digital camera? Haneke has returned to a favorite topos, the relation of reality and visual representation.

As the camera pans across the street, following Georges as he seeks (apparently) to determine whence the original shot was taken, we see a street sign naming the Rue des Iris, which, according to my Parisian street map, places it in the Thirteenth Arrondissement and adds further to the "authenticity" of this shot, at least in terms of its claim to be representing a pro-filmic "real" space. A complete, "realistic" world is formed by suturing the visual and sound tracks: the panning camera head shows Georges speaking as we hear his words, thus lending metalevel credibility to this particular shot.

We cut back to the original shot (we haven't yet learned that it's a videotape), accompanied by their discussion, in voiceover, about what to do with it. A bit of sound editing allows us to hear them moving from one room into the other, "closer" to the image on the screen, and then suddenly we see the fast-forward lines and find out from Anne that the entire videotape—which we understand to be so, for the first time, because of the lines—lasts two hours.

When they spot Georges leaving the house on the video, Georges and Anne rewind and then play the tape at a normal speed, stopping it in freeze frame, while entertaining various hypotheses as to its provenance. (The idea of rewinding itself recalls themes from previous Haneke films, such as the rewinding of the tapes in *Benny's Video*, making the violence they contain, according to Haneke, more "consumable," and the meta-level, self-reflexive rewinding of *Funny Games* that reverses the entire narrative.) We then cut to a metashot of them watching the tape in the quasi-darkness. Naturally, the audience begins to be affected, like the Laurents with whom viewers are starting to identify, with the sense of violation that comes from being watched. As we watch the video intently along with them, we too become investigators of the image (like Georges and Anne) but also voyeurs (like the maker of the tape) as we stare, fascinated, at the video recording their lives. The film analyst watching *Caché* on DVD, rewinding, fast forwarding, and pausing in freeze frame, is of course replicating the same actions as the Laurents, furthering the chain of the *mise-en-abîme* that Haneke plays with here.

The walls of the Laurents' comfortable dining room are covered with books (reminiscent of the pretelevisual epistemological order that obtained in the apartment in *Benny's Video*), as is the set for Georges's television program, which ironically and perhaps anachronistically concerns books. Here on the studio set, however—underlining and complicating the film's theme of the real versus the represented—the books are all fake.

Figure 16. Georges (Daniel Auteuil) moderates his book-discussion show in front of a fake set in *Caché*.

The next time we see a video, or what we learn is a video (we are never told right away), is at night. The shot is apparently from the same angle as the earlier video, and it visualizes the same space and is held onscreen for an extremely long time. A car goes by. Unlike most static long-take images in which "nothing happens," this one compels our attention because a mystery has been provoked by the earlier video, and we wait expectantly for something *to* happen. Suddenly, automobile lights shine brightly as someone pulls up to park in the extreme foreground area that is actually *behind* the camera.

Despite the duplication of the angle and distance, we have no way of knowing whether this shot is "live"—that is, a metashot from the point of view of the director Haneke and his high-definition digital camera making the film called *Caché*—or yet one more video-within-the-film. Importantly, we can never really know because there is no contextualizing or framing shot before or after this one. As Jacques Derrida has pointed out, meaning is always indeterminate because it is finally dependent on context, and context can never be stabilized and fixed. Complicating matters is the realization that whichever of the two it is (Haneke's metafilm or surreptitious video), Haneke and/or his crew have, in any case, shot it, even the video. Our uncertainty about the source of the shot within the fiction leads to a greater and continual uncertainty, at least in terms of a visual epistemology, of the *status* of the shot and its truth value for us as we struggle to construct a meaningful narrative.

It is important, even crucial, to understand that Haneke is not (merely) playing games here. This uncertainty and manipulation regarding the image is central to *Caché* and to his work in general. After the interviewer Richard Porton had quoted to him Godard's famous dictum that "cinema is truth twenty-four frames per second," Haneke replied, "My perspective on that, my article of faith, is that I've adapted Godard's observation to read, 'Film is a lie at twenty-four frames per second in the service of truth.' [Laughs.] Or a lie with the possibility of being in the service of truth. Film is an artificial construct. It pretends to reconstruct reality. But it doesn't do that—it's a manipulative form. It's a lie that can reveal the truth. But if a film isn't a work of art, it's just complicit with the process of manipulation" (Porton 51). It is precisely this question that motivates all the destabilization of the image that occurs in *Caché*.

At his studio, Georges receives another videocassette, this time wrapped inside a child's drawing that shows blood squirting from a child's mouth. The cassette contains the same shot, described in the paragraph above, that we had been watching before we cut to his television show, so only now do we understand its status as another production of the "anonymous stalker," if such a being or entity even exists.

The most important thing here, though, is a strange, brief intercut shot of a small, Arab-looking boy wiping blood from his mouth, clearly connected to the drawing (both of which images we will understand more clearly later) but for which we have at this point no source or even logical motivation. This boy is clearly not part of the present moment. Is this image somehow an untamed emanation from Georges's unconscious that has been released by the drawing and that the metafilm has somehow inserted into the middle of the video? Or is it an interpolated flashback that the viewing of the video has triggered in Georges? In short, what is its status vis-à-vis the present-day tape? (Interestingly, Haneke's careful mise-en-scène has the bloody drawing right next to the television remote control, in a visual field in which virtually nothing else is visible.) Again, Haneke plays with the gap between what we are seeing and the disembodied voiceover provided by Georges and Anne as they, like us, seek to construct a narrative based on the silent images. The "added" image of the Arab-looking boy is a wild card that destroys the internal logic of the videotape that we watch.

When Georges stops the tape, the television image automatically returns to that familiar Hanekean topos, the television newscast, which pursues, automaton-like, its factual recital of mayhem even while the couple continues to talk, leading to a further clash between the competing discourses.

Anne next receives a call in which an anonymous voice demands to speak to Georges, whom we then see—at least his hands, in that familiar Haneke gesture of the visual "cutting off" of body parts—playing with a small card that shows another amateurish drawing of blood spurting out of a child's mouth. When Georges is subsequently almost hit by a bicyclist while getting in his car, a yelling match ensues that Anne is barely able to mediate. It's clear that Georges is beginning to overreact to the pressure of the videotapes and the drawings, and it seems also no accident that the cyclist is a black man, upping the stakes of the conflict, hinting at further complications later in the film, and bringing to bear the modern-day multicultural urban tensions seen in *Code Unknown.*

What next appears is a long shot of students emerging from a school—the same shot, from an identical position, with which the film will mysteriously end. (This repetition later adds to the sense of some unknown third force, someone or something beyond all our possible guesswork who is doing much of the malevolent observing in this film.) A tracking movement centers the figure of Pierrot, the Laurents' son, whose exact role in the film's events remains ambiguous. Once Georges picks him up, Pierrot reveals a card similar to the one Georges has received, but with unexplained indications that it has come from Georges.

Again Haneke plays with our epistemological expectations by making the next shot a long-take on a dark street through an open, second-floor window. We have no way of knowing whether this is simply an informational or traditional establishing shot, a point-of-view shot that will eventually reveal Georges, in a reverse angle, looking at what the shot shows, or yet another anonymous videotape. What follows, apparently "within" this shot, is a strange forward tracking movement on the same dark-skinned child seen earlier, barely visible in the night, coughing

Figure 17. Georges (Daniel Auteuil) loses his cool in multiethnic Paris while his wife Anne (Juliette Binoche) looks on in *Caché.*

and choking from the blood coming from his mouth. Is this a foreshadowing of what we later learn is Georges's troubled childhood, or is it a manifestation of what the film historian Bruce Kawin once called the "mindscreen," or consciousness, of the film itself? Again, there is no way of knowing, either now at the moment of the shot or later, when all the shots have collectively given up all the information they contain.

This forbidding reference to an apparently conflicted past is suddenly replaced by the bright colors of a new day. The dark secrets of the night have been dispersed, and Georges takes Pierrot to school. Interestingly, the shot showing them leaving the house *begins* in exactly the same manner as the first video but then quickly starts to tilt and track, as a—for once—clear-cut marker that what we are seeing emanates from the consciousness of the filmmaker or "external" film, not from a possible video-within-the-film.

The next scene begins with an almost literal shaggy-dog story in which a dinner guest of the Laurents recounts a long tale, which turns into a joke, about something that happened to him. Again, the work any audience must undertake to construct a coherent narrative out of unstable, even invented, material is foregrounded here, just as with the videos. One of the guests, even after the punchline has been delivered to howls of laughter, innocently asks, "Well, was it true or not?"—adding another layer to Haneke's theme. Their further discussion of a friend who is writing a screenplay adds to the sense of self-reflexivity; Haneke keeps us aware that what we watch is always a manufactured and thus manipulated representation.

The doorbell rings, and Georges goes outside to find another tape with an accompanying childlike drawing, this time with the blood shooting from a rooster's cut throat. Angry because Anne tells their friends about the troubling videos and phone calls, he grumpily retrieves the latest cassette he has just hidden in his overcoat, announcing, "I have nothing to hide [*cacher*]." This time the video shows a road, seen through a rain-covered windshield across which wipers move. After a pause, the camera suddenly jerks around to the left to reveal, as Georges explains to his guests, the house he grew up in.

As if the editing, or perhaps the videos, has determined the narrative, rather than vice versa, the next scene depicts Georges visiting his mother in this very house, during which he tells her that he recently dreamed of

Majid. (Could this dream he speaks of be the source of the two intercut moments showing the Arab boy with the bloody mouth?) She seems completely untouched by this information, even though he reminds her that she and his father were once planning to adopt Majid (the child of an Arab family, we learn later, who worked for them). She never thinks about it, she says, because it was long ago, and it was unhappy.

We next cut to Anne at a noisy book party, then suddenly a shock cut takes us to a rooster with its head being lopped off. While the rooster flops around, bright blood splashes on an unknown child's face, which seems to be the bloody face we've seen intercut earlier. At this point we have no idea whether it's a flashback (and if so, whose) or an event taking place in the film's present, but we nevertheless watch horrified as the rooster jumps around headless. The camera cuts several times to a close-up on Georges as a young child, as he is menacingly approached by Majid (whose identity will be verified later) with the hatchet just used on the rooster. Georges, now a grownup, suddenly wakes up, shaken and covered with sweat. The nightmare-sequence is a standard film technique, but in *Caché* it carries an extra bit of anxious resonance because so many of the film's shots lack a clear status and source.

After a short scene showing the present-day Georges walking around his mother's house the next morning, we cut to a shot of a car speeding down a working-class street. Characteristically, the driver is not shown. We are suddenly plunged into the empty hallway of a workers' high-rise building (an "HLM," as it is called in French), and we see only the emptiness in front of the jerky camera, which finally stops at one of the anonymous blue doors. Suddenly, the telltale rewind lines appear, indicating for the first time that, contrary to what we may have thought, we are seeing yet one more anonymous video, and that Georges and Anne are in the process of analyzing it to ascertain the location. Once again, our vision has been tricked, and the ostensibly "self-evident" visual has been shown to be highly ambiguous and difficult to read, especially when decontextualized. This theme, begun with the thriller film that the actress Anne is making in *Code Unknown,* here reaches its apotheosis.

Since they know that the police won't help them, Georges decides to follow the visual clues himself, matching the video markers with the reality that is represented within Haneke's "outer" film. They struggle, with the assiduousness of Antonioni's photographer in *Blow-Up*, to read a street sign. Georges won't tell Anne whom he suspects—Majid, of course, whom we ourselves are beginning to suspect, based on the fragments doled out to us—and they argue about Georges's lack of trust, his absolute refusal to reveal what has been *hidden*, which is an important part of the emotional dynamics of the film and one of its principal themes. Though it's less overtly marked, this theme is perhaps the equal of the reality-versus-representation theme we have concentrated upon thus far and considerably more central to the film than the much-debated historical theme, which will be discussed below. Once again, the audience is forced to laboriously put together clues, in the manner of Georges and Anne, to try to ascertain simply what's in front of them and how it may correspond to some pretextual "real."

Next, we see a stationary shot of the avenue that Georges and Anne have identified, exactly like the many anonymous video clips we have seen thus far. Reversing expectations once again, however, Haneke cuts to a shot of Georges in a café looking out on this avenue, and thus retrospectively motivates the previous shot as a subjective shot, in Haneke's metafilm, from Georges's point of view. Following this, we see the same shot of the empty hallway of the HLM from the point of view of the tracking camera, but this time we hear footsteps that we presume, correctly, are Georges's. (Note the infrequent but important part played by the audio track in sorting out the film's epistemological complexities.) This is verified when we see him walk into the frame and ring the doorbell.

Majid opens the door, and from the very beginning of the encounter between Georges and Majid, it is the former, the privileged one, who is petulant, angry, and aggressive and the latter, the disadvantaged one, who is calm and, initially, even warm and friendly toward Georges. Majid clearly has no idea what has brought Georges to see him. As in *Funny Games*, the motif of the game quickly arises, with Georges saying, like Anna in the earlier film, that because he is now an adult he no longer wants to play. Georges finally says, "You were older and bigger than me, what could I do?" indicating that he knows very well who this man is, but we haven't a clue what Georges is trying to explain. After threatening Majid, Georges leaves. When he calls Anne from a local café, however, he lies to her, for reasons that are, as usual, difficult to divine, and says that no one was home. Clearly he is hiding something once again, something enormous that perhaps we will never fully understand, like so much else connected with this film.

A sudden cut takes us to Pierrot's swimming match, in which a favorite Haneke technique, the tracking camera, is in full operation. Anne and Georges are thrilled when Pierrot wins, and a shot of them cheering also shows many of their fellow observers sporting video cameras, surely a deliberate, even heavy-handed, directorial decision to enhance the scene's self-reflexivity. Another sudden cut takes us *back* to the encounter between Georges and Majid in the latter's apartment, but this time the angle of view is completely different. Again, we are—purposely—confused. Who has taken this shot that lasts longer than the earlier, "real" shot, since it shows Majid sobbing at his kitchen table after Georges has left? What is the status of these images? we ask ourselves once again. Suddenly, we hear Anne say in voiceover, "That's it," and we discover, yet again, that it's a videotape that Georges and Anne have received and are watching.

Georges finally apologizes to Anne for lying about his visit and tells the story of Majid's parents, Algerians who were probably killed in the police massacre of October 17, 1961, when dozens of Arab demonstrators were thrown into the Seine to drown. This historical reference has occasioned, to my mind, a great deal of unwarranted critical speculation to the effect that the film is principally "about" the Algerian War, a great tragedy that has been called France's Vietnam but which is, after all, barely mentioned in *Caché*.

Haneke himself says, in the interview with Cieutat and Rouyer translated for this volume, that "I was still in Austria when I had the idea of doing something about a father and son who were implicated in a sorrowful past. If I had developed it then, I would have interwoven the story with the Second World War. But you can find shadow zones in the past of any country. In regards to France, I had already opted for the Algerian War when I saw, just by chance, a documentary on Arté that really shocked me regarding the events of 1961. . . . Taking Daniel Auteuil's age into account, everything fit. It was not indispensable to the plot, but linking the plot to politics kept the guilt from remaining on the personal level."

"At the same time," he told another interviewer, "I don't want my film to be seen as specifically about a French problem. It seems to me that, in every country, there are dark corners—dark stains where questions of collective guilt become important. I'm sure in the United States there are other parallel examples of dark stains on the collective unconscious (laughs). . . . There's a reason why it's so important to me that this not be seen as a specifically French problem. . . . This film was made in France, but I could have shot it with very few adjustments within an Austrian—or I'm sure an American—context" (Porton 50).

Anne slowly pulls the rest of the story out of Georges: he was jealous of Majid having his own room, so he "told on" him. She pries further, and it turns out that Georges lied about Majid, telling his parents that he had tuberculosis, thus preventing Majid from going to school and getting an education. Georges's central defense, repeated over and over, is that he was only six years old and thus not really responsible for his actions, and that all of the bad things he did were "normal" for a boy of that age. In any case, he terms the affair an "interlude," refusing to see it as a tragedy, thus refusing to show any sympathy for what Majid went through then or in later life. This refusal to recognize a common humanity between him and Majid seems, to Haneke, Georges's greatest transgression. When Anne ejects the new cassette and hands it to Georges, we see that the picture taped to it depicts blood coming from Georges's throat. Haneke's variations on this simple motif, especially one rendered in childlike stick figures, are remarkable.

The refusal to take responsibility for the human tragedy, the blighted life, is demonstrated in the next scene by Georges's superior at the television station, who has also received a copy of the tape and who worries only about the problems the affair could cause for Georges's career, and thus, presumably, his own. Georges lies to him as well, justifying his threats against Majid, captured on the video, by accusing Majid of harboring a supposed "pathological hatred" of Georges's family, of which we have not seen the slightest shred of evidence. Though we will never know for sure, it seems that Georges's own pathological need to lie implies that he is hiding something even more serious than what he has confessed to thus far. Georges returns to Majid's apartment building, and this time the camera *follows* him, a third visual variant for showing the hallway (and for once, narratively clear-cut), but no one is home.

In another signature Haneke gesture, we next cut from a meeting in a café between Anne and their family friend Pierre to a newscast about the war in Iraq, but specific thematic connections with the film we're watching seem remote. The newscast is suddenly contextualized when Anne walks in and we discover that Georges has been watching it on the television in their living room. A serious argument ensues because Anne has turned off her cell phone while out for dinner with Pierre, and the row escalates when they discover that Pierrot is missing.

A trip to the police station results in two officers accompanying Georges down the familiar hallway that leads to Majid's apartment, followed by the camera. As usual, the policemen rough up the Arabs—Majid and his son (Walid Afkir)—solely on the basis of the "Frenchman's" complaint. Humiliatingly, the Arabs are taken to the police station in the back of the police wagon (while Georges sits in the front), as the camera shoots them against the light, clearly suffering, in a purposely dragged-out, quietly intense scene absent of all dialogue.

Pierrot is brought home the next day by the mother of one of his friends, and a battle of wills begins between Anne and Pierrot, who thinks his mother is having an affair with Pierre, which, in light of the final shot of the film, gives some slight reason to believe that Pierrot may himself be engaged in the production of the videos. Yet Haneke structures the film in such a way that we will never know for sure.

After a short, abortive scene in which Georges tries to effect a rapprochement with his alienated son, we cut to Georges's television show, which we naturally take, once again, to be happening live before us, just as we took the earlier videos to be. How many times will we fall for this? Haneke seems to be tauntingly asking. Yet once more it is suddenly revealed that Georges and his producers are in the middle of *editing* the raw video footage of the show, thus again calling into question the epistemological and the ontological status of what we are watching (and what we watch in general). The freeze frame that results is almost shocking when it occurs at the same time as Georges's first, asynchronous voiceover commenting upon what we are watching. Haneke has said that the point of this scene is to critique television by showing that "reality is manipulated by TV to be more attractive to viewers; TV reproduces and transmits a vision of reality that is supposed to be more interesting to viewers, and I am glad I was able to point that out in the film. . . . Yes, absolutely, there is the problem of the terrorism of the mass media today. There is the dictatorship of the dumbing down of our societies" (Badt).

One wonders, though, how many viewers still believe that television shows are unedited, pure reality.

Yet one more trip down the hallway of Majid's apartment building ensues. For once, the camera is at the other end and watches Georges approach the apartment, in what is the fourth or fifth variation of the hallway shot. This gesture also demonstrates the multiple choices (thus, varieties of manipulation) that image makers of any sort have available to them when they purport to show "reality." This time, however, the familiar tracking shot results in the most powerful Hanekean signature moment of all when Majid, ever sweet, ever polite, suddenly cuts his throat in front of Georges, shortly after he has entered the apartment. (The sudden spurt of blood purposely recalls the child's drawings that have accompanied many of the videos, almost as though the action had been preordained.) Georges has entered the apartment throwing his weight around as usual, only to be instantly defeated by the most powerful statement available to the powerless. Georges is completely frozen, and the full meaning of Majid's gesture cannot and will never be made clear, to him or to us.

But Haneke rejects the false clarity of "the powerful versus the powerless" opposition as an explanation for the relation between Georges and Majid. He told Porton, "I'm not sure if it's so black and white. We don't know if Georges is telling the truth, and we don't know if Majid is telling the truth. We don't really know which one of the characters is lying—just as we don't know in real life. You can't say that the poor are only poor and good and the rich are only rich and evil. Life is far more complex, and as a filmmaker and artist, I'm trying to explore the complexities and contradictions of life. I hope that, for that reason, the film is unsettling and disturbing—mainly because we don't know how to react" (Porton 51). This theme—the final, fundamental unknowability of reality and character psychology—has been regularly sounded by Haneke at least since *The Seventh Continent*.

Uncharacteristically, Haneke is more willing to speculate on the reasons behind Majid's desperate act itself: "I think his suicide represents a couple of things. First of all, it's a desperate act of self-destruction. But it's also an act of aggression directed toward Georges. Interestingly, someone I know who saw the film recently recounted to me a story that he had heard. A man who had left his wife was asked by her to meet him at a subway station. They met and, while he was there, she threw herself under a subway car before his eyes. I think that's an interesting comment on my film" (Porton 51).

After Majid's abrupt suicide, Georges, seriously distraught, leaves the apartment and goes to the movies to avoid having to go home. Finally, he enters his dark house from the rear, using his cell phone to ask his wife to get rid of their dinner guests. Again, he wants her to lie to them, to hide something from them, which she is reluctant to do, but ultimately he reveals more details to her of the truth of his childhood with Majid.

Another long shot out Georges's bedroom window, like the one earlier, leads us to wonder, once again, about its motivation—we have become so epistemologically paranoid—though the source is revealed as Georges, who is looking out the window while walking around in the dark. Anne slowly drags more hidden information out of her husband in a scene that takes place in the dark room, against whose windows, through which only the slightest bit of light passes, the two figures seem virtually hidden. He keeps trying to avoid, to hide, the whole truth, making us suspect that perhaps there is even more to the story that we will never learn. He gives more details about lying to his parents about Majid coughing up blood, which fits perfectly with the blood motif that has structured the film, then about lying to Majid by telling him that Georges's father wanted Majid to kill the rooster, whence the blood that drenches Majid in Georges's earlier nightmare-sequence.

From the dark hiddenness of the bedroom, we cut to the incredibly bright, high-tech modern building that houses Georges's studio and the channel's administrative offices. It stands in contrast to everything that has gone before, especially the shabbiness of Majid's apartment. Here, unlike Georges's past, apparently everything is transparent, open, unhidden. Suddenly Georges is confronted by Majid's son, who wants to talk to him. When he threatens Georges with making a scene by telling everyone things they shouldn't hear, Georges says he has "nothing to hide." Majid's son is polite, like his father, though decidedly more assertive, yet he seems merely to want some expression of sympathy from Georges, which the latter—as always, presuming himself as utterly guiltless, with "nothing to hide"—refuses to give. Majid's son denies any involvement with the videos, yet Georges once again refuses to believe his and his father's denials no matter how convincing they may seem to us.

Majid's son seems most interested in making Georges face all the repercussions of his childish actions: "You deprived my father of a good education. The orphanage teaches hatred, not politeness, but my Dad raised me well." Georges's self-defensive response: "I refuse to have a bad conscience because your dad's life was miserable. I'm not responsible." And, once again, Georges threatens him, as he has threatened his father on several other occasions. Majid's son, however, gets the last word before he leaves: "I just wondered how it feels to have a man's life on your conscience. That's all. Now I know."

We cut to the same shot of the outside of the Laurents' house, from the same angle, with which the film begins. At this point, thoroughly schooled in the instability of the image, we wonder what the status of the shot is. One of the things suggested here is that whoever is the author of the videos, he or she is still at work. Or perhaps that it is "Haneke" who has been the real author of the videos—which, of course, in a practical sense, he is, since he or someone under his direction shot them to make this film we're watching. In any case, the shot of the outside of the house turns out not to be another surreptitious video but part of the "outer" metafilm.

Georges pulls up, parks the car, and goes into the house, announcing to his wife over the phone that he has taken "deux cachets." (One wonders if the second word, "pills," a homonym for the film's title, is being used on purpose.) He is enveloped by the same deep blue color that we have seen in so many of the earlier films, and he goes to bed. The complete darkness that he achieves by closing the blinds suggests, symbolically perhaps, that much remains hidden in his mind and conscience.

This unconsciously self-defensive action on the part of Georges seems to represent the central moral point of the film for Haneke, since he discusses it at great length in an interview.

> The moral question the film raises is how to deal with this question of guilt. All of us have moments of selfishness, moments that we prefer to hide. The Daniel Auteuil character has this choice. The act that he carried out may not be likeable, may be reprehensible, but it is realistic, all of us have these hidden moments in our lives . . . we all feel guilty, about the relationships between the industrialized world and the third

world, or how we deal with the elderly, for example. We all take sleeping pills as does Daniel Auteuil, although it may take many different forms: it may be alcohol, a drink before we go to bed, it may be sleeping pills, or we may donate money to children in the third world. But each of us pulls the blanket over our heads and hopes that the nightmares won't be too bad. For example, I am sure you oppose strict immigration laws that have been introduced in almost every European country. And yet what would you say if I were to suggest that you take into your home an African family? I think this is the case with all of us. All of us have knowledge that tends to lead to tolerance; at the same time we have selfish interests that are contradictory to this tolerant ideal. (Badt)

After Georges takes the sleeping pills, we cut to a powerful, lengthy scene in which Majid is being cruelly taken away from Georges's house sometime during the 1960s. Again we are unsure of the shot's status, but this time for a different reason. Is it Georges's dream or merely an autonomous flashback, as it were, the film's mindscreen or "memory"? The camera rigorously holds on an extreme long shot, and everything plays out at a distance, all perfectly framed. In its immobility, it recalls the shot of the Laurents' house that opens the film. We also remember the scene of the killing of the rooster, since the camera occupies the same position as it did in that scene, though this time the central action plays out much further away. After Majid tries to run away (toward the camera) from the people who are taking him away to the orphanage and is captured, the car finally drives off, and the scene is again silent. We do not see Georges waking up, which would contextualize or motivate the scene as his dream.

When Haneke was asked by Cieutat and Rouyer why he chose to show this flashback, when it was already understood from the story itself, he replied, "It's one thing to know something and another thing to feel it. I find that scene very touching. I didn't put it in earlier because I wanted to save it for the end: Daniel's character takes his two sleeping pills, pulls the covers over his head, and hopes to escape, but the reality is something completely different."

Instead of seeing Georges wake up, we cut to the final and most inexplicable scene in the film. It is the same shot that we have seen earlier, when Georges arrives to pick up Pierrot at his school. This time, however, we clearly see Majid's son and Pierrot talking in the upper left-hand corner with a group of Pierrot's friends. Majid's son, much older than the others, seems out of place. They then move down the steps, just the two of them, to the lower left-hand portion of the screen—the camera doesn't budge—and while Majid's son gesticulates expressively, he continues to look suspiciously all around him as though he might soon be caught. When they part, Majid's son seems to be smiling.

Does this, looking to the past, mean that Pierrot and Majid's son, each for his own reasons, have been partners in the making of the disturbing tapes? Or, looking to the future, does it mean that Majid's son is now planning to exact his revenge on Georges for his father's suicide by first befriending his son? Even more complexly, what is the status of this shot, and what chronological place does it occupy? (Just because it comes last in the film chronologically does not mean it happened last, just as the previous scene is actually something that took place forty years earlier.)

We finally see Pierrot, now alone, go back up the steps and talk to some other friends—perhaps to finalize the details of a plot?—then they all come back down the steps and depart screen left. At the same second that Pierrot disappears from the visual field, the final credits begin to roll. As the film ends, we not only have no idea "whodunit"; we're not even sure about exactly what has been done.

Many critics and some ordinary viewers I've spoken with have criticized the director for not sorting out everything by the end of the film. For this viewer, however, the indeterminacy of the ending feels right and is a powerful indicator of how seriously Haneke takes his work. One makes films in the service of art, not to satisfy audiences, he would insist. In fact, it's perfectly obvious that we never fully comprehend the world or why people do the things they do, so why should we expect a film to lie to us and say that we can?

Caché, for all its inexplicable mystery, demonstrates that Haneke has not strayed far from the themes and obsessions with which he began his remarkable cinematic journey. As in all the films from *The Seventh Continent* on, he is still thinking about the meaning and instability of representation and the way cinema must always manipulate the audience by purporting to show, or at least to tell us something about, reality, including the reality of violence. But it is larger than that, as well, because the real fault of the media, defined as broadly as possible, is that if it is not acting in the service of art (that is, not continually seeking to shake us out of our reassuring slumber), it is putting us more deeply to sleep. And it is in this sleep, with the covers pulled over our heads, that we can refuse to communicate, and thus refuse to recognize our own guilt and, most important, our common humanity, for Haneke, the greatest sin of all.

The White Ribbon (2009)

Haneke's most recent film, as of this writing, is *The White Ribbon*, which won the Palme d'Or at the 2009 Cannes Film Festival. It's a brilliant, richly achieved work that is superbly acted, a masterpiece of historical reconstruction as well as a powerful sociohistorical critique, and it demonstrates clearly the director's ongoing ability to surprise. Taking what may be only a temporary break from his French-language films of the past decade, Haneke is once again working in German. Even more surprisingly, *The White Ribbon*, whose script, Haneke said at the Cannes press conference,[12] he has been working on for ten years, is set in the early twentieth century—though we only find out exactly when, crucially, late in the film—despite the fact that none of his previous films, with the possible exception of part I of *Lemmings* (which was made in 1979 and set in 1959), is a period piece.

Besides the film's narrator, who is also the local schoolteacher, the cast of characters includes the Baron, his Steward, the Pastor, the Doctor, the Midwife, and the Farmer—plus all their assorted spouses and children—as well as a governess named Eva, who has caught the eye of the Schoolteacher, and several other minor characters. This use of generic roles rather than proper names has the effect of making the film more overtly abstract and symbolic, clearly one of Haneke's principal goals. It also emphasizes the rigid social structure that obtains in the village, which has nothing to do with individual personalities and everything to do with social roles.

Other surprises include the fact that the film is narrated in voiceover—a technique unheard of in Haneke's previous work—years after the events depicted take place. (Sony Pictures Classics, the film's American distributor, says that the voiceover will be translated into English for its release in the United States, to my mind a wise choice.) It's also shot, again for the first time in a Haneke film, in black and white, marked by rigorous and thematically fitting compositions, a visual choice that is stunningly appropriate for the time period in which the film is set. Many gorgeous shots (winter snow scenes, buildings presented straight-on and perfectly framed, blowing wheat, the stark interior of the village church) demonstrate a concern for aesthetic beauty that is present but subdued in his earlier films.

Perhaps Haneke is finally beginning to fear less the power of the image, and thus allowing himself to exploit it more. When asked why he used black and white, he said that it was mainly because our image of that period tends to be in black and white (unlike earlier centuries, which we know through the color of paintings, and the following century, which we know through color photographs and films). Color, he said, would have lessened the possibility of making the depicted reality more purposefully abstract. This decision accords with the distancing achieved by the voiceover narration and the generic roles of the principal characters. Significantly, Haneke also said that he used black and white because "I love it."

And though the various stories with which the film is occupied are told in rather short vignettes, the fades to black that punctuated earlier films are now gone. In their place is the bookend structure of a fade-up from gray at the beginning of the film and a fade-down to gray at the end. There is no music, except of the diegetic variety, as when the Schoolteacher plays the organ, the Baroness plays Schubert on the piano, and the choir sings in the church.

In a similar vein, Haneke has taken great care to make the individuals seem as "authentic" as possible, particularly by making the characters, especially the children, closely resemble photographs of the period, which is where our visual knowledge of the era comes from. According to the director, some seven thousand children were considered for the children's roles, with the first criterion being acting ability but the second being that of an authentic look that we unconsciously associate with the period. The costumes are also perfectly appropriate, and great care has obviously been taken in their regard. A like touch comes in the extremely simple credits—tiny white words against a black background—when the German words for "A German Children's Story" are written in by hand, as it were, under the words of the film's title. The letters are in the handwritten script version of the Black Letter or Gothic font that was the standard form of the German language at the time.

One of the biggest changes is how refreshingly straightforward the film is. While its plot is centered around a mystery (whose solution is purposely obvious almost from the beginning), unlike in earlier Haneke films, we almost always know exactly what is going on in each scene, who the various characters are and how they are related to each other, despite—or perhaps because of—the very large cast. Similarly, while the film's pacing is deliberate—Haneke hasn't changed everything—it seems always to be moving toward a clear, predetermined goal. Close-ups dominate, even extreme close-ups, and Haneke's signature tracking shot is seldom if ever utilized. Long-takes appear only occasionally, as when he holds on an empty, silent hallway for what seems at least a minute, until we hear the sounds of a child being beaten behind the closed door of another room.

On the surface, the film tells a fable-like tale of the interpersonal dynamics of a conservative turn-of-the-century Protestant community somewhere in northern Germany. At this initial level, up through the first half of the film, say, we are privy to the unexceptional personal lives of the village's denizens, ruled by its rigid social hierarchy. Haneke's focus on the supposedly unimportant everyday features of his characters' lives is no different from many of his earlier films. However, he also holds out the promise of something more, something deeper, when he inserts, in the narrator's initial voiceover, the words, "I believe I must tell of the strange events that occurred in our village, because they may cast a new light on some of the goings-on in this country."

In other words, the particular is given the resonance and importance of the universal from the beginning of the film. The "strange events" referred to are a series of suspicious accidents and several anonymous child beatings. The Doctor's horse is tripped up by a hidden wire, sending him to the hospital for months, and the Farmer's wife is killed in an accident in the lumber mill. Sigi, the young son of the Baron, is severely whipped by unknown persons, and later Karli, the "mongoloid" illegitimate son of the Midwife, is beaten nearly to death. The Baron's barn is also set on fire, and his cabbage patch is shredded.

As these events—some of which are unrelated and obvious in their intention, while others remain unexplained—begin to slip out of the community's collective mind over time, Haneke probes more deeply, and we start to see the reality behind the carefully constructed façade of this God-fearing community. Thus we discover that the Doctor is sexually abusing his fourteen-year-old daughter and psychologically abusing his mistress, the Midwife. At one point, his verbal attack on the Midwife, while she is masturbating him, is so vicious ("Your breath stinks, and you are old and ugly. Why don't you just die?") that it constitutes violence of the most unmitigated sort. The Pastor, an upright, fearsome figure who recalls some of Bergman's more rigid clerical characters, is so incensed about his son Martin's proclivity toward masturbation (which he can only speak of in the most roundabout way) that he ties his hands to the bed at night. Martin and his sister Klara are also forced to publicly wear the "white ribbon" that betokens purity and innocence—which, according to their father, they have yet to achieve. His other children are regularly sent to bed without dinner after each has shown obeisance by kissing the Pastor's hand. He so humiliates Klara during confirmation class at the school that she passes out, and the Steward brutally canes his son for taking another boy's cheap flute. The children of the Doctor unhealthily discuss death at great length, and Klara, the daughter of the Pastor, stabs a pet parakeet and leaves it dead on her father's desk. The desperate husband of the woman killed in the Baron's unsafe lumber mill hangs himself, because his son's futile gesture of revenge (destroying the Baron's cabbage patch) has caused the Baron to discharge the Farmer, in effect starving his large family. Yet occasional acts of tenderness also occur, as when the Pastor pauses for a moment, obviously moved, over the unexpected kindness of one of the children he tyrannizes in the name of "good discipline." But any such inadvertent demonstration of human feeling is quickly repressed.

It is only at the very end that we find out, via the stunning announcement that Archduke Ferdinand of the Austro-Hungarian empire has been assassinated in Sarajevo, that the film is set on the verge of World War I. In the meantime, the Schoolteacher deduces that the various outrages committed against the village, at least the ones that remain unexplained, have been instigated by the children, who seem to have morally run amuck despite—or because of—the severe discipline they have had to endure. The Baroness, who wants to leave her husband, makes one of the few overt denunciations by a character in the film when

Figure 18. Martin (Leonard Proxauf) wears his badge of shame in *The White Ribbon*.

she tells the Baron that she can no longer stand him or this horrible village, which is rife with "malice, envy, and brutality."

The village's enthusiasm for the coming war erases all previous scandals, and the narrator's last words are, "Today, more than a quarter of a century later, toward the end of my life, and several years after the end of a second war that was to change this world in a more cruel and radical way than the first one, the one we faced at the time, I wonder if the events of those days and our silence about them weren't the germ of the tragedy toward which we were heading. Didn't we all know secretly what had happened in our midst? Hadn't we, in a way, made it possible by closing our eyes? Didn't we keep our mouths shut because otherwise we would have had to wonder if the misdeeds of these children, of our children, weren't actually the result of what we'd been teaching them?"

The film ends with a series of three shots perfectly framing the church, each one at a greater distance, as though the director were moving toward an ever greater sense of abstract universality. Then we cut to another perfectly square, rigorously framed shot of the interior of the church and hear the choir, which occupies the upper quarter of the unchanging shot, singing sweetly as the Pastor takes his place. The image fades back to gray, and the film ends.

Haneke has purposely avoided any precise delineation of the film's sociohistorical critique, but it seems clear that it's meant to be a portrait of German society prior to the beginning of World War I, with a hint of the fascism to come. But he also insisted that he wasn't only, or even, offering an analysis of the origins of fascism, as one might conclude because the film is set in Germany. No, he insisted, as he had earlier about the supposed "Frenchness" of *Caché*, this problem concerns everyone and in every nation, and perhaps now more than ever.

For Haneke, the central moral lesson of the film is that if children have absolute values impressed upon them, especially with violent reinforcement, they will absorb these values and act the same way in their turn. "Anytime you have absolute principles, this leads to terrorism of many different kinds. Absolute principles always become inhuman." He also mentioned that the original title of the film was "The Right Hand of God," since if children are told repeatedly that a certain system of values is always correct, then they will act to punish the others who don't follow the rules precisely or who don't fit the approved template (like the Doctor, Sigmund, and Karli), just as they themselves were violently punished, presumably for their own good.

What is most fascinating here is that Haneke's interests and themes seem to have come full circle, returning to his earlier, brilliant television films like *Lemmings*, to trace the causes for the wars and dislocations of German-speaking countries back to the social and familial structures, as well as the accompanying, often violent value system, that obtained at the time. *Lemmings* as well offered an analysis of sorts of the disillusioned, even suicidal youth who committed petty crimes just for the thrill of it in reaction to the bourgeois values of their World War II–era parents.

Gone therefore—at least for the moment—is the critical examination of the media, of Hollywood manipulation of the audience, of the power of the image, and of the audience's moral responsibility, all themes that have played such a huge part in the films made for theatrical release, beginning with *The Seventh Continent* in 1989. Now back in the sociopolitical, historical analysis where his career began, it is difficult to say whether this represents a true break and return for Haneke, or merely a temporary respite. Yet one thing remains, and that is the director's ongoing, tireless investigation of the ills of our society, past and present—that sick society, of which we are all a part, that keeps us from ever being fully human to one another. As he gleefully said at the end of the Cannes press conference, "My films are like a ski jump—and it's up to the spectator to take off!"

Notes

1. For further discussion of Haneke's television films, see Brunette, "Michael Haneke and the Television Years."

2. See the two interviews in this volume for specific details regarding Haneke's working methods and how his various cinematic techniques are achieved.

3. It is important to note that Haneke does not see a clash between opera and punk rock in the film. "I have nothing against popular music and wouldn't think of playing popular against classical forms. I'm very skeptical of the false conflict that already exists between so-called 'serious' music and music categorized strictly as entertainment. . . . But, of course, with the guessing game at the beginning of the film there is an irony in the way their music suggests their deliberate isolation from the exterior world, and in the end they are trapped in a sense by their bourgeois notions and accoutrements, not just by the killers alone" (Sharrett).

4. Haneke's view of *A Clockwork Orange* is similar. "I'm a huge Kubrick fan, but I find *A Clockwork Orange* a kind of miscalculation, because he makes his brutality so spectacular—so stylized, with dance numbers and so on—that you almost have to admire it. . . . I read somewhere—I'm not sure if it's true—that Kubrick was completely shocked when he saw how the public reacted to *A Clockwork Orange,* and he even tried to have the film recalled. It became a cult hit because people found its hyperstylized violence somehow cool, and that was certainly not what Kubrick had intended" (Wray 49).

5. To quote from the section on the works of the Marquis de Sade: "Reason is the organ of calculation; of planning; it is neutral with regard to ends; its element is coordination. More than a century before the emergence of sport, Sade demonstrated empirically what Kant grounded transcendentally: the affinity between knowledge and planning which has set its stamp of inescapable functionality on a bourgeois existence rationalized even in its breathing spaces. The precisely coordinated modern sporting squad, in which no member is in doubt over his role and a replacement is held ready for each, has its exact counterpart in the sexual teams of Juliette, in which no moment is unused, no body orifice neglected, no function left inactive" (69).

6. One can only imagine the toll that this film took upon the actors. As Haneke tells Toubiana, "As always, I work very technically. For example, the long scene after the death of the child. I went into their wardrobe and talked about all the emotional stages. I was saying, 'Take your time to put yourself in the situation.'

We were in the studio, everything was ready, they came in and did the scene twice, and at the end, no one could speak, it was so strong. But when he forces her to pray, for example, that was very hard because she couldn't reach that level of feeling. So we shot that scene over and over, maybe twenty-eight times, and at the end she was totally exhausted, and then it worked. But we needed someone who had the will to do this. Because I know few actors or actresses who would dare to go as far as she did in the film, physically as well. Her eyes were all swollen, and it wasn't makeup."

7. In a curious sense, this story may already have been made in the United States in a 1955 film called *The Desperate Hours*, directed by William Wyler and starring Humphrey Bogart, who plays a sociopathic criminal. It's a taut, extremely well-made thriller about three escapees from prison who terrorize a family (father, mother, young boy, and teenaged girl) in their own home over a period of several excruciating days. Many of the themes that show up in *Funny Games* are already present in this fifty-year-old film, such as the focus on the daughter's vulnerable sexuality, the psychological castration of the father figure (Frederic March), and the sense of the "invasion" by unsavory elements of the sanctity of middle-class life, embodied in the home. Most strikingly, at one point the mother (Martha Scott) accuses the Bogart character of gratuitous "torture and cruelty"—that is, beyond what is necessary for a successful escape from prison—and even refers to his continual brutality as "some kind of game." The principal differences are that in the earlier film the police play an important role, there is much attention paid to class resentment and only a small amount of violence, and, most importantly—and unsurprisingly for a Hollywood film— the family is saved in the end.

8. When asked by Dave Calhoun why he remade the film, Haneke agreed that it had always been at least partially directed to an American audience, especially given the fact that the violence of American movies led him to make it. "The title was an English title. If you look closely at the inside of the house in the original, there's no house like this anywhere in Austria! The idea of the original was to address the American viewer of violent films a little bit, but unfortunately because of the German-speaking cast, the original film worked only on the art-house circuit. When they gave me the opportunity to make it again and in a new language, I said, 'Okay, let's do it.' I hope it works. We'll see. I'm very curious" (Calhoun).

9. During the period in which Haneke was making films for theatrical release, he also made an excellent adaptation of Franz Kafka's *The Castle* (1997), which also starred Ulrich Mühe. This film will not be discussed in the present book, principally because of Haneke's own rigid distinction: "I would draw a definite line between *The Castle* and *The Piano Teacher*, because *The Castle* was made for television, and I'm very clear about the distinction between a TV version and a movie. Films for TV have to be much closer to the book, mainly because the objective with a TV movie that translates literature is to get the audience, after

seeing this version, to pick up the book and read it themselves. My attitude is that TV can never really be any form of art, because it serves audience expectations. I would not have dared to turn *The Castle* into a movie for the big screen; on TV, it's OK, because it has different objectives. But with *The Piano Teacher*, if you compare the structure of the novel to the structure of the film, it's really quite different, and I feel I've been dealing very freely with the novel and the way it was written" (Foundas).

10. Haneke has said that "Isabelle represents both sides of the character: she has this extraordinary emotional strength and capacity for suffering, but also this icy intellectualism. If I was to shoot this film, she had to play the role" (Applebaum).

11. Music offers a rich subtext in this film that unfortunately, owing to limitations of space and the present author's lack of musical expertise, cannot be fully explored here. There is also an important socioaesthetic aspect. Haneke told Sharrett that "you need first to understand that in that film we are seeing a very Austrian situation. Vienna is the capital of classical music and is, therefore, the center of something very extraordinary. The music is very beautiful, but like the surroundings it can become an instrument of repression, because this culture takes on a social function that ensures repression, especially as classical music becomes an object for consumption. Of course, you must recognize that these issues are not just subjects of the film's screenplay, but are concerns of the Elfriede Jelinek novel, wherein the female has a chance, a small one, to emancipate herself only as an artist."

As Haneke told another interviewer, however, "I present music as a form of pure beauty. But it is also true that, in this Viennese petty bourgeois society, music allows people to rise socially. . . . However, the social reality doesn't detract from the beauty. It is like trying to analyse love: you can try to define it as a physiological process, but that doesn't touch the reality of the emotion that affects people. Music, in my opinion, is the most sublime art of them all" (Applebaum).

12. All of Haneke's remarks concerning *The White Ribbon* are taken from this press conference, held on May 21, 2009.

"Interview with Michael Haneke:
The Fragmentation of the Look"

Interview by Michel Cieutat, translated from the French by Peter Brunette. (Originally appeared in *Positif* 478 [December 2000]: 25–29.) Interview conducted at Cannes, May 20, 2000; translated from the German by Robert Gray.

MICHEL CIEUTAT: [*Code Unknown*] is the second time, after *71 Fragments of a Chronology of Chance*, that you've opted for a story based on a structured fragmentation. You seem very interested in this narrative mode.

MICHAEL HANEKE: For me, it's not an interest but rather a necessity because the cinema of distraction [Haneke's term for Hollywood or any non-art film] claims that we can show reality in its totality, which is false. If the cinema wants to be responsible—in other words, a true art—it's obligated to realize that our perception of the world is naturally fragmented. So we have to find the aesthetic means that will allow us to transfer this fragmented look onto the screen. Today no writer would dare claim that he or she could retranscribe the totality of the world in a book. He or she too would think about the means of writing that would lead him or her to reproduce this same fragmented perception of existence. It's an attitude that is certainly not particular to the modern world—it's always been that way—but we're more conscious of it in our time. It's my personal way to proceed. It's not a fascination for fragmentation: it results very naturally from the force of this necessity.

MC: It's also in addition a major common theme of your films, this loss of the sense of reality from which Western man suffers today.

MH: Yes. I belong to a generation that was able to grow up without the continuous presence of television. I was thus able to apprehend the world directly, without an intermediary. Today, on the other hand, children learn to know reality through films, and reality is presented on television in two different ways: there is the reality of documentary shows and the reality of fictional images. I think that the media has played an important role in this loss of the sense of reality, but that isn't the only reason. In the industrial world in which we live, the one I make my films for, we are also participating in a refusal of reality. For example, we don't want to recognize whatever we don't like. So we construct interior walls that are psychological or spiritual.

MC: What is the source of the screenplay for *Code Unknown*?

MH: There were several things that led me to that scenario. First of all, a call from Juliette Binoche, who wanted to work with me, then the idea that I had to make a film on the theme of immigration, on the opposition between the rich people of the host country and the poor people who go to this country, a contrast that can only continue to grow during the course of the new century that is about to begin. I had noticed that there were two cities where you could begin to see the putting into place of this type of multicultural society: London and Paris. When I got the call from Juliette, already having this subject on my mind, I saw an interesting coincidence there, and I decided to make the film in Paris, where I had been doing research for several months. I met with people from the black community, clandestine Romanian immigrants—whose problems I already knew a little bit about, since I treated them in a character in *71 Fragments*; then I went to Austria to assemble . . . my material! But that only concerned the material level of the film—its story, its plot. The major point of the film went beyond the immigration theme.

MC: Do you remember the first fragment [of your material] that showed up in the screenplay?

MH: No, because I take a lot of notes; but the day comes when I feel that I have enough, and then I proceed to a kind of a big collage. Each idea is written on a sheet of paper, and I assemble the ideas on a big table. It's the longest and most necessary work. The general structure is everything for me. The writing of the screenplay itself goes quickly. It's easy to write a scene when you already know the context. As far as writing the dialogue, it's a pleasure and goes even more quickly! The construction of the whole is much more complicated and takes time. Besides, I never start writing until I have the entire structure in my head. For [*Code Unknown*], I in fact started with the first scene that you see, but I no longer remember the first fragment I kept.

MC: During the editing, did you change the order of the appearance of the fragments vis-à-vis the screenplay?

MH: Yes, there were several changes, because during the shooting, we realized that the final amount of footage was going to be longer than we had thought. So four scenes that were in the script disappeared: two were abandoned because we already knew that the film would be at least two hours long, but they weren't absolutely fundamental scenes; and, also before shooting, there were two scenes that I thought were flawed and weren't necessary either! But then I had to restructure the whole thing, not a lot, but still a little bit. Since that time, I've forgotten what exactly.

MC: This writing in articulated fragments around a certain number of characters links your film to a subgenre called the "choral film." But *Code Unknown* seems different somehow.

MH: *71 Fragments* and *Code Unknown* are different from *Short Cuts, American Beauty*, or *Magnolia*, a genre that's currently in vogue. These films have a tendency to tie up the strings of all their stories at the end. After finishing *71 Fragments*, I tried to do the opposite, or something much more complicated. I prefer to follow all the strings, in perfect continuity, without losing them, but without ever having to come back to them to tie them up in an explanatory way. That was my biggest worry during the elaboration of the structure of *Code Unknown*. It's very difficult to tell a story in that way.

MC: Your use of the long-take implicates the spectator on the level of identification with the protagonists and on the level of his or her manipulation by the director. In other words, is the long-take just as much an affair of realism as a calling into question of the reality shown?

MH: I used the long-take in *Code Unknown* for several reasons. First, in order to find a rigid structure for the fragments, as in a puzzle, but also to separate them from the scenes relating to the film-within-the-film, which are shown in the usual way. Another reason was to let each scene develop in real time, which is a way of not manipulating time; which is also a kind of manipulation, because it's a question of showing that the scenes of the film-within-the-film are just as artificial as the other sequences. In fact, in *Code Unknown,* everything goes back to manipulation. I play with that, because everyone knows that cinema is a manipulation of the spectator; and it's not a question of knowing it but of feeling it, of understanding it more deeply. Whence the difference in the way the two types of scenes were handled. Besides, people mix them up. The scene in the swimming pool, for example, which was edited in the normal way, was taken by many people for a real scene in the film. I also wanted to show, starting with these two opposed aesthetics, that spectators taken by a well-made story can be totally manipulated . . . as I wanted them to be!

MC: But one can feel oneself more implicated than manipulated, for example, in the scene in the subway, which could be taken for a real, contemporary document.

MH: That's not contradictory. To create an artificial universe, one always develops a situation in which one is implicated, which is the danger the cinema represents: you can make people believe they are implicated in a situation to the point where they're no longer capable of judging things coldly, of remaining outside. That's what most of the filmmakers who play on identification do. I, on the other hand, am always fighting a little bit against this idea of identification. I give the spectator the possibility of identifying, and immediately after, with the help of the black shots for example, I say to him or her: Stop a little bit with the emotional stuff and you'll be able to see better!

MC: How do you prepare your long-take shots?

MH: It's much more difficult than normal shooting, but I had very good actors, an excellent assistant, Alain Olivieri, who made my task easier with numerous extras, for example, during the second sequence (in the street) and the one in the restaurant. For the scene in the street, we had three days: one for rehearsing the actors with the camera, one for placing the extras in relation to the camera, and one for the shooting. There were thirty-two takes. Actually, we interrupted several of them as soon as a problem arose. Nevertheless, we were able to shoot eight or nine complete takes. The worst was making the definitive choice, because naturally we never had a perfect take. The beginning shot was best, so we had to choose that take, but there were errors as well. . . . As always, I worked a lot on the sound, and I kept the sound from another take and then stuck it on the one that was kept. For the sequence in the restaurant, we had one day of rehearsal and one day of shooting during which I shot thirty-three takes! For the sequence in the subway, everything had to go very fast, because we couldn't start until after midnight, and we had to stop at 4:00 A.M. We had to do everything in the space of two or three hours. It was hard! But I have to say that I had worked a lot with the two young men beforehand: we had rehearsed before the shooting, as early as the auditions, then during weekends, because they were nonprofessionals. The young Arab, Walid Afkir, is extraordinarily talented. We found him totally by chance on the street.

MC: Tell us about the black caesuras between the fragments.

MH: They were already in *The Seventh Continent* and *71 Fragments*. These "black shots" are directly linked with the different sequences. They create a real sense of fragmentation. In *The Seventh Continent*, their duration corresponded to the depth of the preceding scene. If there was a lot to think about in the sequence, I made the black last longer. [In *Code Unknown*,] as in *71 Fragments*, they are all two seconds long. Unfortunately, the projectionists don't always respect them when they're at the end of a reel and even elsewhere: in many festivals, they just cut them right off, except at the Directors Fortnight at Cannes! I had to put a little explanatory text on each reel! To come back to the fragmentation, I also opted for other little things, like cutting during the dialogue: in the scene of the letters from the photographer, the reading is interrupted right in the middle of a word; in other sequences, a question is barely asked before the cut comes and excludes the answer. A total reality can never be captured in the cinema or in real life. We know so little!

MC: Since *The Seventh Continent*, your way of putting a film together, at first very close and understated, very Bressonian, has gotten progressively expanded from film to film.

MH: In *The Seventh Continent*, I examined the objectification of our lives, which are now determined by a whole series of givens. That implied the use of a precise aesthetic. I was very well aware of the fact that a close-up has a different meaning in film and in television. But the succession of very closely linked shots not being very common on television, that led me to think that it was the appropriate discourse to convey this concept of the objectification of the individual. I came back to this aesthetic with *71 Fragments*: there's a connection between this film and *The Seventh Continent*, just like between *Benny's Video* and *Funny Games*, which take up a certain thematic. There is always a tight relation between the content and the form. Consequently, I am never devoted to a single, specific aesthetic. But I think that, whatever the style that is chosen, you can still recognize my films!

MC: How do you develop your sound track?

MH: The sound track is already more or less established in the screenplay. I even write the sounds in capital letters to distinguish them from the rest, which is written in lowercase letters. I try to describe them as precisely as possible, but while shooting, everything depends on the physical context that is created by the actors, their movements, and the sounds that result. I treat the sounds just like the images and handle them in such a way that the final result corresponds to what I had planned. That said, sound represents a different kind of work than that on the image: there are things that you don't manage to record, so we have to find something else.

MC: How do you direct your actors?

MH: It's difficult to say. But, as always in my work, the finished film corresponds absolutely with the screenplay: I draw a storyboard, and nothing is added during the shooting, with the exception of what the actors bring to their characters from their own personalities, from their sense of creativity. What's most important for the actors is the mutual trust that creates a feeling of security for them. That way, an actor can go much further than he or she would otherwise. People had already asked Fred

Zinnemann, a filmmaker of Austrian origin, how he got the actors in his films to perform so well. He replied that it had to do with two things: good casting and the fact that all mistakes had to be avoided! It's a philosophy that I subscribe to. As far as my particular way of working with actors goes, I am very tenacious, and I keep doing takes until the actors give me what I want. I can't compare my work with that of other directors, because I don't have the slightest idea how they work. But the thing that I'm most sure about is that you have to love actors. I love them a lot.

MC: A very strong sequence in *Code Unknown* is the one that shows the photographer, in the subway, who is stealing the passengers' portraits.

MH: Those are photographs taken by Luc Delahaye, a well-known war photographer who is also a friend of mine. I met him through Raymond Depardon, whom I know well, and who had the idea of making a film on a war correspondent. The war correspondent, whom I don't know, had written a text that Depardon had given me because, in the meantime, he had given up the project. I was interested in a character who was a photographer who specialized in war photography because it allowed me to integrate another reality by means of his photos. Then Luc gave me a book of photos that he had taken in the subway, and I found the idea extraordinary for the film. We thought of having him retake the photos, but that would have produced photos consciously taken and would have been totally different. It's better to photograph beings who aren't conscious of having their picture taken. One should reproduce, but create.

MC: Where does the title come from?

MH: From the first impression I had felt in Paris, that one couldn't go anywhere without knowing the code number of a building. And for me that was a very good first image in terms of the film's contents. Like the preface you find before beginning a novel that tells you that, without the proper code, you won't be able to figure out the feelings you're going to be confronted with: you are going to stay outside, and there won't be any communication. So it's a title that has two meanings.

MC: What is your interpretation of the drumming scene—as much paradoxical as cheerful—given by the group of deaf people (deaf people create sounds with the greatest joy), in relation to the title, *Code* (one uses a code to protect oneself better) *Unknown* (but without the code one no longer can communicate)? Isn't art the only thing left as the last great refuge for man?

MH: Yes, I think so. Art is the only thing that can console us whatsoever! But spectators have to look for their own responses wherever they are. It's useless if they find responses that don't come from within. That can only give them a good conscience.

MC: You've studied philosophy. Has that had a direct influence on your films?

MH: No, I don't think so. Like all young people who study philosophy, I was looking for answers to questions that preoccupied me. But, as you quickly find out, philosophy doesn't offer any solutions. So I can't speak of a philosophical influence on my work. At the time, there were people who influenced me, like Hegel, because my professor was a Hegelian; for him, in fact, philosophy more or less ended with Hegel. In our studies we got as far as the Viennese Circle, but without really going very deeply. Like all artists, I think that Wittgenstein influenced me a great deal, but not in the sense that one tries to appropriate the world, but rather that, as he said himself, it is better to be silent than to try to express the inexpressible. It's the mystical aspect of Wittgenstein's thinking that especially attracted me.

MC: When did your interest in the various destructive processes that afflict man begin?

MH: I think that I am someone who is creative and sensitive to every form of suffering. I can't stand suffering, and that might explain it. Actually, I have difficulty identifying the reasons that have led me to write my stories. I find myself in the position of the centipede who's been asked how he manages to walk: he's then incapable of moving! However, that makes me think of Wim Wenders's film *The End of Violence*, which begins by trying to define violence. I myself have asked that question, and the answer that I found is that violence is the ultimate recourse of power against the will of others who must then be subjected to it.

MC: One very upsetting aspect of your previous film, *Funny Games*, was that the two torturers imposed their power on their victims by means of a process of making them feel guilty. When a code becomes unknown, isn't that the same process?

MH: The theme of guilt is present in all my films. *Funny Games* was meant as a metaphor for a society that has turned inward and excluded the exterior world. Men today live in prisons they've created for themselves. They can't escape, because they're the ones that built the walls that surround them. So it's their own fault. This is where the feeling of guilt that every victim feels comes from. There is no victim in my films who is completely innocent. But nevertheless, these victims aren't killed because of their guilty feelings. In *Funny Games* I was playing with an ironic contradiction: each one of my victims became guilty of a reprehensible act before the torturers took over. Of course, they were forced by the two young men to act that way, like the mother who suddenly isn't polite any longer, the father who slaps one of the young men, or the son who is the first to shoot. It was an ironic way of keeping spectators from siding with the victims right away because they sympathized completely with them. I was also trying to draw the attention of the audience to the fact—in terms of criminal violence—that things in the world aren't so simple. Obviously, there's no connection between the guilt of these people and their final disappearance. It's not some kind of punishment; that would be completely idiotic to think that.

MC: In fact, you are exploring the absurd as applied to the world of violence and noncommunication?

MH: Yes, it's very Kafkaesque. Guilt is the first question in all of Kafka's works. It's also true of all my films, including *The Castle*, of course! It's inherent in our Judeo-Christian tradition and especially in Central Europe. Actually, in all of the West.

MC: Your liberal opinions are well known, as well as your opposition to Jorg Haider [the late Austrian right-wing politician], and yet some have called *Funny Games* a fascist film. What is your response?

MH: You can't make a film against fascism using an aesthetic that is itself fascist. It's the same thing with violence. You can't make a film against violence using a style that is found in films of violence. For *Funny Games*, I therefore had recourse to a fairly large number of means that allow spectators to be conscious of what is happening, to understand the actions and the gestures of the characters. The film could never be fascist or Nazi, because Nazism consists essentially in violating people to take something away from them. If my film were fascist, it would violate the thoughts of others. Those who call my film a Nazi film are those who don't want to understand this phenomenon of guilt that we just spoke of. Guilt that applies equally, during the projection, to the spectators. But maybe these people just don't want to understand!

**"Interview with Michael Haneke:
You Never Show Reality, Just Its Manipulated Image"**

Interviewed by Michel Cieutat and Philippe Rouyer, translated from French by Peter Brunette. (Originally appeared in *Positif* 536 [October 2005]: 21–25.) Interview conducted at Cannes, May 15, 2005.

MICHEL CIEUTAT and PHILIPPE ROUYER: *Caché* seems to take us back to an earlier period in your work, after a parenthesis constituted by *The Piano Teacher* and *Time of the Wolf*.

MICHAEL HANEKE: It's true, these two films are a little bit apart, resurrected from my past. I had written *The Piano Teacher* for an Austrian colleague who wanted to shoot it with an American actress. But after ten years he still hadn't managed to get the project going, and the producer finally asked me to direct it. I really didn't want to because it wasn't a personal story. But because I didn't have anything else available to shoot very quickly, I finally agreed on the condition that Isabelle Huppert play the principal role. She was ideal for the part. I had written *Time of the Wolf* earlier, just after *The Seventh Continent*. At the time, it was an hour longer. It started in the city and was a big futurist film. After September 11, I told myself that the moment had come to pull it out of the drawer, because the events had given it a new relevance. In fact, this time I got financing.

MC and PR: How far back does the project for *Caché* go?

MH: I wrote it after *The Piano Teacher*. September 11 convinced me to insert the shooting of *Time of the Wolf*, but I still took the time to finish the screenplay of *Caché* first. I would have liked to shoot it in 2004, but we couldn't find the money. We had to give up the idea of a French production and make it an international production instead in order to get the necessary funds. So I put almost four years into getting this project finished.

MC and PR: What was its origin? The desire to return with Juliette Binoche after *Code Unknown* back to Paris?

MH: No, it was the desire to make a film with Daniel Auteuil. I had met him through my press attachée, Matilde Incerti, and he had confirmed that he wanted to work with me. So then I started thinking about what I could come up with for him.

MC and PR: What did you find interesting in him?

MH: In addition to his great talent, he has something that fascinates me. It's like a secret, something inside him that pushes us to ask ourselves what there is behind him. In an earlier time, Jean-Louis Trintignant had the same hidden thing.

MC and PR: How did you use this secret in terms of his character?

MH: It just worked on its own. I didn't have anything to add. Sometimes it's like that, when the casting is good. When people tell me my actors are always good, I quote Fred Zinnemann, the Austrian filmmaker who had his career in Hollywood and who said, "In order to make a good film, there are two things to respect: get a good cast and don't make any mistakes!" A good cast doesn't only mean having good actors but having good actors in roles that have a close connection to them. And I think that worked very well with Daniel Auteuil in *Caché*.

MC and PR: Were you thinking of the Algerian War right from the beginning?

MH: No. I was still in Austria when I had the idea of doing something about a father and son who were implicated in a sorrowful past. If I had developed it then, I would have linked the story with the Second World War. But you can find shadow zones in the past of any country. In regards to France, I had already opted for the Algerian War when I saw, just by chance, a documentary on Arté that really shocked me regarding the events of 1961. I asked myself how, in a country in which discussions regarding political conflicts had always been so open, it was possible that no one was talking about these two hundred deaths in Paris. Taking Daniel Auteuil's age into account, everything fit. It was not indispensable to the plot, but linking the plot to politics kept the guilt from remaining on the personal level.

MC and PR: Can you tell us about the last two shots that sum up the whole film? One is a flashback, and the other projects us into the future, giving us to understand that no one, across time, can ever escape the feeling of guilt.

MH: We're all the inheritors of sins committed by our parents, and of their . . . non-sins! Unfortunately that's how human existence goes. It's unavoidable.

MC and PR: Why did you actually show the flashback, since it was already known through the history itself?

MH: It's one thing to know something and another thing to feel it. I find that scene very touching. I didn't put it in earlier because I wanted to save it for the end: Daniel's character takes his two sleeping pills, pulls the covers over his head, and hopes to escape, but the reality is something completely different.

MC and PR: Do you put everything together right after writing the script?

MH: I always make a storyboard before shooting. But the choice between a fixed shot and a long-take shot [in which the camera follows the action] is decided earlier, during the writing. So it was always clear in my mind that the final two shots were fixed and that they would refer back in their framing to previous shots (the nightmare with the chicken). It's often the structure of the scene that demands a certain form, like the shot/countershot for the argument between the mother and the son. But it also depends on the locations you find. For this film, I had the luck to shoot all the interior shots of the house in a studio. We could really do exactly what we wanted because we had set up the decor to meet our needs.

MC and PR: How did you work with your cameraman, Christian Berger, regarding the light and the white highlights? Did you give him specific instructions from the beginning?

MH: In fact, even if we changed the details considerably, we conceived the decor by being inspired by the real interiors of the house that was shot for the exteriors. I had found that house by accident when we passed it on our way to look at another house. It attracted me immediately because of its situation in the street, almost hidden by the other buildings that are behind it. In terms of my script, filming this house amounted to showing the part for the whole because it represents a place where one feels well protected. The white came from its luxurious 1930s, art-deco aspect. In addition, this very real house also had an artist's studio that was very practical for diffusing a neutral and even lighting on the whole decor. As soon as I saw the house from the outside, I understood what I could get out of it for the lighting.

MC and PR: The paradox is that this neutral and diffused light creates an unquiet climate right from the start. . . .

MH: If you had had a very dramatic kind of lighting, that would have been too forced. You always have to work against the expectations of the audience. And you have to hide what you want to show in order for it to work.

MC and PR: At the same time, there's no space to hide in this house, because the light is so pale. . . .

MH: Yes, but the house claims to protect because there are no windows. In an apartment with windows, you can be filmed from outside. Here, it's impossible. Yet the characters are still being watched.

MC and PR: But the observing comes from the inside. The effect is obvious in the scene in which Bénichou cuts his throat, because the angle of the shot. . . .

MH: It's the same as in the shot where he's shown on the television. It's just a little bit off because the background wasn't really parallel.

MC and PR: The spectator is even more confused because there's no space to allow the intruder to film Bénichou, taking into account the closeness of the wall. . . .

MH: If you could search the frame, you would see that a little camera has been placed there, against that wall, hidden right in the middle of all the clutter. A camera put there by anybody. But it's there! You could even think that the whole suicide is also a trick!

MC and PR: Tell us about the texture of the film, which was shot in high-definition digital, which allows one to put the real and its representation on the same level.

MH: I wanted to have that video texture in order to destabilize his control of the immediate reality. That caused us a lot of problems with material because, today, the video cameras, it's horrible: they make noise because of the fan in the computer, which turns faster as the computer heats up. We also had problems with the calibration: there are many fewer colors than with film, and that quickly becomes horrible. I swore to myself that my next film would not be in video! In *Caché*, it was necessary for the story, but the technical side is not right. Even if I know that it's the future. In fifteen years, we'll only be shooting in video!

MC and PR: That said, here, it's thanks to that digital texture that, after having been tricked from the opening sequence, we become very vigilant at the sight of the slightest fixed shot!

MH: You've become poisoned then! So much the better! But this little game is not something new for me. I did something similar in *Funny*

Games. Because all those claims today to want to show reality really bother me. You never show reality; you only show its manipulated image.

MC and PR: There's also, as in *Funny Games*, the idea of the absolute power of images and of the filmmaker who produces them over those who look at them. . . .

MH: Yes, but to get where? That's the question.

MC and PR: Let's ask you that question.

MH: To make you realize that you are being manipulated. With no matter what film, you're being manipulated, but people are dishonest enough never to say it. I, on the other hand, show it to say it. I think it's the exact opposite position. You can't escape this problematic: as soon as you make a frame, it's already a manipulation. I just try to do it in a transparent manner.

MC and PR: However, you leave a little bit more freedom to the spectators than your fellow filmmakers, in that you use music less?

MH: Yes, because that really bores me. I love music too much to use it to cover up my mistakes! In film, it's often used this way, no? Besides, in a "realist" film, where does the music come from, excluding the times when it comes from a radio that's been turned on? Now, in my film there are no situations in which one would be listening to music. And I would have found it dishonest to try to cover up mistakes.

MC and PR: Why, after *Funny Games*—which, to our minds, had already magnificently explored this theme—did you feel the need to return to the denunciation of the power of images?

MH: Because I think that you have the obligation to do it in every film. Today, if you are a writer and if you are serious, you wouldn't dare claim that you can describe reality in all its complexity. That means that you are thinking in the work itself about the impossibility of description. And, in my opinion, the cinema is obligated to do the same thing. If not, it's still in the nineteenth century. But it's reassuring that even the current mainstream cinema works and makes its money that way. Now, if cinema wants to be an art, it must find the means that lead to other reflections. That's why I love the work of Kiarostami, who pleased me enormously when he came to see my film and confided to me as he was leaving, "That's my Golden Palm!" I think that he's the greatest because he too constantly explores the same subject. And he is pushing the reflections to the highest levels that one can today.

MC and PR: Your film deals with a unique and difficult theme for almost two hours. How do you manage to keep your spectators in suspense? Do you try to multiply the false digressions, like the story that Denis Podalydes tells against the background of a set (the real library in the dining room), which later will be taken up again (a fake library) on the stage of the literary show of Daniel Auteuil?

MH: It's like the Russian dolls, the doll inside the doll inside the doll. For me, making references and going back to things that have already happened is an artistic pleasure. It's not absolutely necessary, but it enriches the dramatic construction. It's like a musical fugue. Of course, one can do the music differently, but the doubling of the theme brings in more complexity and pleasure.

MC and PR: Where does the story told by Podalydes come from?

MH: I was at a party where someone told it. I liked it so much that I took notes on it while telling myself that I would use it one day. Here, it fits well with what's going on because you're wondering if it's true. All the while realizing, with the black woman who says so aloud, that it's a stupid question. Besides, Denis tells the story beautifully, which was very difficult in a single shot. He had two pages of text to say while raising the comic tension. I had planned to shoot some reaction shots of the people listening in case he couldn't pull it off. But he's a very good actor, and he told it as I had hoped. So I was able to stay with the wide shot.

MC and PR: Did the film change a lot during the editing, especially in the length of the long-take, moving shots and the [long-take] fixed shots?

MH: It wasn't possible for the long-take, moving shots, where you have a certain timing you have to respect during the take. In traditional editing, you can always change the shots that don't work, even throw them away. But with the moving long-take shots and the fixed shots, you can't fix things in the editing. That's the danger. On the other hand, I edit very quickly, in three weeks. Editing the scenes in shot/countershot takes more time because it gives you more options. With the moving long-take shots as well, you have to choose, but it's always more difficult because in these five- to eight-minute shots, there are always, depending on the takes, some moments that are less good and others that are better. So you have to choose between two possibilities, and you always lose something. It's heartbreaking. I adore postproduction, but I hate having to make these choices!

MC and PR: In a fixed shot like during the credits, you can still play with the length during the editing. . . .

MH: No, the timing was very precise for this shot. It's the same principle as for 71 *Fragments of a Chronology of Chance*. I know that the audience has understood the shot after ten seconds and is waiting for the next shot. But when it keeps going, they become upset, then angry. You have to plan for all that in advance while working. I have to know how I would react if I were the spectator. It's the director's job to have an interior sense of timing to know how it's going to be received by the audience. If, for example, you have a shot on a house, it's very important to decide when a car or a person is going to pass in front of it. A little bit earlier or a little bit later, it might not work as well. It's very delicate point to explain. It's a question of breathing. So it's very important to work with someone on the editing who *breathes* like you. The female editors that I work with make the cuts at the moments I want them to. That's why I say that the cinema is closer to music than to literature.

MC and PR: When do you calibrate this timing? During the rehearsals, just before the takes? Speaking more generally, do you do a lot of rehearsing?

MH: Yes, we rehearse a lot for the fixed shots and the moving long-take shots. It's inevitable. The worst are the moving long-take shots, because the camera also has to function in relation to the whole, which is sometimes very difficult for the actors. For example, for the shot in which Daniel Auteuil returns from the police station and begins to cry at the end of it: because of the different entrances into the house, it was horrible because of the digital camera, which is never really in focus. We had to do it over and over again, for at least three quarters of a day, to get it to work technically. In addition, we had five actors, and one of them hesitated. It was much more complicated than if it had been filmed in shot/countershot. In that case, we would have shot it three times from that angle, three times from the other angle, and that's all—we could have gone straight to editing.

MC and PR: How many takes on average are there for a single moving long-take shot?

MH: You can end up doing a lot of them. In general, it goes from three to thirty! It depends so much on little things that you can never imagine how many takes you're going to need. With the shot I was just describing, we had a problem that cost us a half a day. The camera was supposed to enter the kitchen ahead of Daniel, and a tiny little difference between the tiled flooring of the kitchen and the carpet of the living room messed us up. To this was added another problem caused by the door, which we couldn't get the camera through. We had to open it to let the camera in and, immediately afterward, halfway close it again before Daniel came in. These are really shitty little things, but necessary for the shot to work.

MC and PR: During the shooting of a long-take shot, if you notice a mistake made by one of your actors, do you stop the take or continue?

MH: You don't always know because you have to be attentive to a thousand things at once. During the take, I look at the actors above all, and I don't bother about the camera. Then I look at the video recording, and sometimes I don't notice something that's gone wrong. So I look at it several times. For that, video is a real gift! Without being able to check it on video, I would never have filmed the moving long-take shot of *Code Unknown* on the street. Quite simply because you can't watch two hundred people at the same time to make sure that no one is looking at the camera. That said, it happens from time to time that you will interrupt a long-take that has started badly. Especially if you've already done twenty takes, because it's very tiring for the actors. If I feel that things are beginning to drag, to lose intensity, I call a coffee break to recuperate. But most often it's the camera that causes the interruptions.

MC and PR: Where are you during the takes?

MH: Always in front of the actors, with headphones for the sound, because if you're far away from them, you can't hear very well. It's only after the take that I go check to see what's on the computer drive.

MC and PR: Without the actors?

MH: Oh, yes! From time to time they want to look, but I ask them not to. If, in spite of everything, they insist on looking at their performance, I let them. They are professionals, and they know what they are doing. But with young actors or people with less experience, I never allow them to watch. That would be too destabilizing for them because they wouldn't be seeing the film in its entirety, but only themselves. It wouldn't be right to reproach them for this, because it's only natural. As soon as you appear in an image, you are looking at yourself.

MC and PR: Why did you opt for widescreen (1/1.85), which corresponds to the 16/9 ratio of [widescreen] television. Does that interest you?

MH: I wanted a frame that corresponds to today's television. It wouldn't have worked with real Scope. But it all depends on the story. I have no particular predilection for one format over another. I would have loved to have shot at least once in 1.33, but that's no longer possible nowadays.

MC and PR: Are you thinking of beginning another film in French?

MH: No, I have a German-language project that I wrote four years ago. A film on the youth of the years 1913–14, the generation that would become Nazis twenty years later. This will be a three-hour film with a lot of people in it, sketching a portrait of a German village via its nobility, a grandfather at the head of his company and his little workers. But, of course, everything depends on the success of *Caché*. If I can't manage to get this project going, I have another one that is more modest. Since it's not yet written, I can't speak about it in detail. All that I can say is that it's a contemporary subject with few characters and that it's in French.

MC and PR: Are you now perfectly integrated into French cinema and society?

MH: Yes. Which gives me the privilege of being able to create in two different countries. That allows me to work continuously, and it's very nice.

Note: Only the films extensively covered in this book, those made for theatrical release since 1989, are listed here.

The Seventh Continent (Der siebente Kontinent, 1989)
Austria/Germany
Production Company: Wega Film
Director: Michael Haneke
Writers: Michael Haneke and Johanna Teicht
Producers: Veit Heiduschka
Cinematographer: Anton Peschke
Music: Alban Berg
Editor: Marie Homolkova
Production Designer: Rudolf Czettel
Art Director: Rudolf Czettel
Costume Designer: Anna Georgiades
Cast: Dieter Berner (Georg), Udo Samel (Alexander), Leni Tanzer (Eva), Birgit Doll (Anna)

Benny's Video (1992)
Austria/Germany
Production Companies: Bernard Lang and Wega Film
Director: Michael Haneke
Writer: Michael Haneke
Producers: Veit Heiduschka, Michael Katz, Bernard Lang, and Gebhard Zupan
Cinematographer: Christian Berger
Editor: Marie Homolkova
Production Designer: Christoph Kanter
Set Decorator: Christian Schuster
Costume Designer: Erika Navas
Cast: Arno Frisch (Benny), Angela Winkler (Mother), Ulrich Mühe (Father), Ingrid Stassner (Young Girl)

71 Fragments of a Chronology of Chance (71 Fragmente einer Chronologie des Zufalls, 1994)
Austria/Germany
Production Company: Wega Film
Director: Michael Haneke
Writer: Michael Haneke
Producers: Veit Heiduschka and Willi Zegler
Cinematographer: Christian Berger
Editor: Marie Homolkova
Production Designer: Christoph Kanter
Costume Designer: Erika Navas
Cast: Gabriel Cosmin Urdes (Marian Radu, Romanian Boy), Lukas Miko (Max), Otto Grünmandl (Tomek), Anne Bennent (Inge Brunner), Udo Samel (Paul Brunner), Branko Samarovski (Hans), Claudia Martini (Maria), Georg Friedrich (Bernie)

Funny Games (1997)
Austria/Germany
Production Company: Wega Film
Director: Michael Haneke
Writer: Michael Haneke
Producer: Veit Heiduschka
Cinematographer: Jürgen Jürges
Editor: Andreas Prochaska
Production Designer: Christoph Kanter
Costume Designer: Lisy Christl
Cast: Susanne Lothar (Anna), Ulrich Mühe (Georg), Arno Frisch (Paul), Frank Giering (Peter), Stefan Clapczynski (Georgie)

Code Unknown: Incomplete Tales of Several Journeys (Code inconnu: Récit incomplet de divers voyages, 2000)
France, Germany, Romania
Production Companies: Bavaria Film, Canal+, Filmex, France 2 Cinéma, Les Films Alain Sarde, MK2 Productions, Romanian Culture Ministry, Zweites Deutsches Fernsehen (ZDF), and Arté France Cinéma
Director: Michael Haneke
Writer: Michael Haneke
Editors: Karin Hartusch, Nadine Muse, and Andreas Prochaska
Producers: Yvon Crenn, Marin Karmitz, and Alain Sarde
Cinematographer: Jürgen Jürges
Production Designer: Emmanuel de Chauvigny
Set Decorator: Laurence Vendroux

Costume Designer: François Clavel
Original Music: Giba Gonçalves
Cast: Juliette Binoche (Anne Laurent), Thierry Neuvic (Georges), Josef
    Bierbichler (The Farmer), Alexandre Hamidi (Jean), Maimouna Hélène
    Diarra (Aminate), Ona Lu Yenke (Amadou), Djibril Kouyaté (The Father),
    Luminita Gheorghiu (Maria), Bruno Todeschini (Pierre), Walid Afkir (The
    Young Arab), Maurice Bénichou (The Old Arab)

The Piano Teacher (La Pianiste, 2001)
Austria, France, Germany
Production Companies: Arté, Bayerischer Rundfunk (BR), Canal+, Centre
    National de la Cinématographie (CNC), Eurimages, Les Films Alain
    Sarde, MK2 Productions, P.P. Film Polski, Wega Film, Österreichischer
    Rundfunk (ORF), and Arté France Cinéma
Director: Michael Haneke
Writer: Michael Haneke, from the novel by Elfriede Jelinek
Producers: Yvon Crenn, Christine Gozlan, Veit Heiduschka, and Michael
    Katz
Music: Francis Haines
Cinematographer: Christian Berger
Editors: Nadine Muse and Monika Willi
Production Designer: Christoph Kanter
Set Decorator: Hans Wagner
Costume Designer: Annette Beaufays
Cast: Isabelle Huppert (Erika Kohut), Annie Girardot (The Mother), Benoît
    Magimel (Walter Klemmer)

Time of the Wolf (Le Temps du loup, 2003)
France, Austria, Germany
Production Companies: Bavaria Film, Canal+, Centre National de la
    Cinématographie (CNC), Eurimages, France 3 Cinéma, Les Films du
    Losange, Wega Film, and Arté France Cinéma
Director: Michael Haneke
Writer: Michael Haneke
Producers: Veit Heiduschka, Michael Katz, Margaret Ménégoz, and Michael
    Weber
Cinematographer: Jürgen Jürges
Editors: Nadine Muse and Monika Willi
Production Designer: Christoph Kanter
Art Director: James David Goldmark
Costume Designer: Lisy Christl
Cast: Isabelle Huppert (Anne Laurent), Béatrice Dalle (Lise Brandt), Patrice

Chéreau (Thomas Brandt), Maurice Bénichou (M. Azoulay), Olivier Gourmet (Koslowski), Brigitte Rouan (Béa), Lucas Biscombe (Ben), Hakim Taleb (Wild Child), Anaïs Demoustier (Eva)

Caché (Hidden, 2005)
France, Austria, Germany
Production Companies: Les Films du Losange, Wega Film, Bavaria Film, BIM Distribuzione, France 3 Cinéma, Arté France Cinéma, Eurimages, Centre National de la Cinématographie (CNC), and Canal+
Director: Michael Haneke
Writer: Michael Haneke
Producers: Andrew Colton, Valerio De Paolis, Veit Heiduschka, Michael Katz, Margaret Ménégoz, and Michael Weber
Cinematographer: Christian Berger
Editors: Michael Hudecek and Nadine Muse
Production Designers: Emmanuel de Chauvigny and Christoph Kanter
Costume Designer: Lisy Christl
Cast: Daniel Auteuil (Georges Laurent), Juliette Binoche (Anne Laurent), Maurice Bénichou (Majid), Annie Girardot (Georges's Mother), Bernard Le Coq (Georges's Editor-in-Chief), Walid Afkir (Majid's Son), Lester Makedonsky (Pierrot Laurent)

Funny Games (U.S.; 2007–8)
United States
Production Companies: Celluloid Dreams, Halcyon Pictures, Tartan Films, X-Filme, Lucky Red, and Kinematograf
Director: Michael Haneke
Writer: Michael Haneke
Producers: Christian Baute, Chris Coen, Hamish McAlpine, and Andro Steinborn
Cinematographer: Darius Khondji
Production Designer: Kevin Thompson
Art Director: Hinju Kim
Set Decorator: Rebecca Meis DeMarco
Costume Designer: David C. Robinson
Cast: Naomi Watts (Anne), Tim Roth (George), Michael Pitt (Paul), Brady Corbet (Peter), Devon Gearhart (Georgie)

The White Ribbon (Das weisse Band, 2009)
Germany, Austria, France, Italy
Production Companies: X Filme Creative Pool (Berlin), Wega Film (Austria), Les Films du Losange (France), and Lucky Red (Italy)
Director: Michael Haneke

Writer: Michael Haneke (Jean-Claude Carrière, consultant)
Producers: Stefan Arndt, Veit Heiduschka, Margaret Menegoz, and Andrea
    Occhipinti
Cinematographer: Christian Berger
Editor: Monika Willi
Production Designer: Christoph Kanter
Sound: Guillaume Sciama and Jean-Pierre Laforce
Costume Designer: Moidele Bickel
Cast: Christian Friedel (The Teacher), Leonie Benesch (Eva), Ulrich Tukur
    (The Baron), Ursina Lardi (The Baroness), Fion Mutert (Sigmund),
    Burghart Klaussner (The Pastor), Steffi Kühnert (Anna), Maria-Victoria
    Dragus (Klara), Leonard Proxauf (Martin), Josef Bierbichler (The
    Steward), Gabriela Maria Schmeide (Emma), Janina Fautz (Erna), Rainer
    Bock (The Doctor), Roxane Duran (Anna), Miljan Chatelain (Rudolf),
    Susannne Lothar (The Midwife), Eddy Grahl (Karli), Branko Samarovski
    (The Farmer).

Bibliography |

Applebaum, Stephen. "Michael Haneke: *The Piano Teacher*" (interview). October 30, 2001; December 27, 2007. http://www.bbc.co.uk/films/2001/10/30/michael_haneke_interview.shtml.

Arthur, Paul. "*Hidden:* The Paranoid Universe of Michael Haneke." *Film Comment* 41.6 (November/December 2005): 25–28.

Badt, Karin. "Family Is Hell and So Is the World." *Bright Lights Film Journal* 50 (November 2005); December 27, 2007. http://brightlightsfilm.com/50/hanekeiv.htm.

Baudrillard, Jean. *Simulacra and Simulation.* Trans. Sheila Faria Glaser. Ann Arbor: University of Michigan Press, 1994.

Brunette, Peter. "Michael Haneke and the Television Years: A Reading of *Lemmings.*" In *A Companion to Michael Haneke.* Ed. Roy Grundmann (Oxford: Blackwell Publishing, forthcoming).

Calhoun, Dave. "Michael Haneke: Interview." *Time Out London.* December 27, 2007. http://www.timeout.com/film/features/show-feature/3658/michael-haneke-interview.html.

Cieutat, Michel. "Entretien avec Michael Haneke: La fragmentation du regard." *Positif* 478 (December 2000): 25–29. (Translation reprinted in this volume.)

Cieutat, Michel, and Philippe Rouyer. "Entretien avec Michael Haneke: On ne montre pas la réalité, juste son image manipulée." *Positif* 536 (October 2005): 21–25. (Translation reprinted in this volume.)

Combs, Richard. "Movie of the Moment: *The Piano Teacher.*" *Film Comment* 38.2 (March/April 2002): 26–28.

DeBord, Guy. *The Society of the Spectacle.* Trans. Donald Nicholson-Smith. New York: Zone Books, 1994.

Derrida, Jacques. *Limited Inc.* Ed. Gerald Graff. Trans. Jeffrey Mehlman and Samuel Weber. Evanston, Ill.: Northwestern University Press, 1988.

Edelstein, David. "Audience is Loser in Haneke's Unfunny 'Games.'" National Public Radio, March 14, 2008; August 30, 2009. http://www.npr.org/templates/story/story.php?storyid=88230619.

Falcon, Richard. "Forbidding Cinema: The Discreet Harm of the Bourgeoisie." *Sight and Sound* 8.5 (May 1998): 10.

Foundas, Scott. "Interview: Michael Haneke, the Bearded Prophet of *Code Inconnu* and *The Piano Teacher*." December 4, 2001; December 27, 2007. http://www.indiewire.com/article/interview_michael_haneke_the_bearded_prophet_of_code_inconnu_and_the_piano1/.

Frey, Mattias. "A Cinema of Disturbance: The Films of Michael Haneke in Context." *Senses of Cinema* (August 2003); December 27, 2007. http://sensesofcinema.com/contents/directors/03/haneke.html.

———. "Supermodernity, Capital, and Narcissus: The French Connection to Michael Haneke's *Benny's Video*." December 27, 2007. http://cinetext.philo.at/magazine/frey/bennys_video.pdf.

Fuller, Graham. "Shots in the Dark: When Directors Tackle Their Own Remakes, Who Scores?" *Interview* 38.1 (February 2008): 64.

Grossvogel, David I. "Haneke: The Coercing of Vision." *Film Quarterly* 60.4 (Summer 2007): 36–43.

Grundmann, Roy. "Auteur de Force: Michael Haneke's 'Cinema of Glaciation.'" *Cineaste* 32.2 (Spring 2007): 6–14.

Heidegger, Martin. "The Question Concerning Technology." In *The Question Concerning Technology and Other Essays*. Trans. William Lovitt. New York: Harper and Row, 1977. 3–35.

Horkheimer, Max, and Theodor W. Adorno. *Dialectic of Englightenment: Philosophical Fragments*. Ed. Gunzelin Schmid Noerr. Trans. Edmund Jephcott. Stanford, Calif.: Stanford University Press, 2002.

Jeffries, Stuart. "No Pain, No Gain." *The Guardian,* May 24, 2001; December 27, 2007. http://www.guardian.co.uk/culture/2001/may/24/artsfeatures.

Jelinek, Elfriede. *The Piano Teacher*. Trans. Joachim Neugroschel. New York: Weidenfeld and Nicolson, 1988.

Kawin, Bruce. *Mindscreen: Bergman, Godard, and First-Person Film.* Princeton, N.J.: Princeton University Press, 1978.

Le Cain, Maximilian. "Do the Right Thing: The Films of Michael Haneke." *Senses of Cinema* (May 2003); July 13, 2006. http://archive.sensesofcinema.com/contents/03/26/haneke.html.

MacNab, Geoffrey. "Funny Games." *Sight and Sound* 11.4 (April 2001): 63.

Morrow, Fiona. "Michael Haneke: All Pain and No Gain." *The Independent,* November 2, 2001; December 27, 2007. http://arts.independent.co.uk/film/features/article_142008.ece.

Porton, Richard. "Collective Guilt and Individual Responsibility: An Interview with Michael Haneke." *Cineaste* 31.1 (Winter 2005): 50–51.

Price, Brian. "Pain and the Limits of Representation." *Framework* 47.2 (Fall 2006): 25.

Rhodes, John David. "Haneke, the Long Take, Realism," *Framework* 47.2 (Fall 2006): 18.

Scott, A. O. "A Vicious Attack on Innocent People, on the Screen and in the Theater." *New York Times,* March 14, 2008; April 5, 2008. http://movies.nytimes.com/2008/03/14/movies/14funn.html?pagewan.

Sharrett, Christopher. "Austria, The World That Is Known: Michael Haneke Interviewed." *Kinoeye: New Perspectives on European Film* 4.1 (March 8, 2004); December 27, 2007. http://www.kinoeye.org/04/01/interview01.php.

Time of the Wolf. DVD. Palm Pictures, 2004.

Toubiana, Serge. Interview with Michael Haneke. *Benny's Video.* DVD. Wega Filmproduktion, 1992. Kino International, 2006.

———. Interview with Michael Haneke. *Funny Games.* DVD. Attitude Films and Fox Lorber Home Video, 1998.

———. Interview with Michael Haneke. *The Seventh Continent.* DVD. Wega Filmproduktion, 1989. Kino International, 2006.

———. Interview with Michael Haneke. *71 Fragments of a Chronology of Chance.* DVD. Wega Film, Camera Film, ZDF/Arté, 1994. Kino International, 2006.

Vicari, Justin. "Films of Michael Haneke: The Utopia of Fear." *Jump Cut* 48 (Winter 2006); December 27, 2007. http://www.ejumpcut.org/archive/jc48.2006/Haneke/text.html.

Vogel, Amos. "Of Non-Existing Continents: The Cinema of Michael Haneke." *Film Comment* 32.4 (July/August 1996): 73–75.

Wood, Robin. "Hidden in Plain Sight: Robin Wood on Michael Haneke's *Caché.*" *ArtForum* 44.5 (January 2006): 35–37.

Wray, John. "Minister of Fear." *New York Times Magazine,* September 23, 2007, 44–49.

Wyatt, Jean. "Jouissance and Desire in Michael Haneke's *The Piano Teacher.*" *American Imago* 62.4 (Winter 2005): 453–82.

136n3, 138n11; narrative devices, 10; responsibility of audience, and the, 7; sound, use of, 144; sudden violent gesture, use of, 27, 85–86, 125; television, 3, 8–9; violence in films and media, 2, 5–7, 11. *See also specific films*

Heidegger, Martin, 47–48

Horkheimer, Max, 62, 64–65

Jelinek, Elfriede, 4, 88

Kawin, Bruce, 119

Lacan, Jacques, 54, 96

Lane, Anthony, 70

Le Cain, Maximilian, 46

Lemmings (1979), 3, 130, 135

Magnolia (Anderson), 44

Natural Born Killers (Stone), 58–59

Once Were Warriors (Tamahori), 56

Piano Teacher, The (2001), 88–103, 110, 148; as literary adaptation, 88–91, 92, 93–94, 95–96, 98, 100, 102, 138n9; as pornography, 90; shift to character psychology in, 91

Red Desert (Antonioni), 14, 106

Sade, Marquis de, 136n5

Schindler's List (Spielberg), 6

Scott, A. O., 6, 70–71

Scream (Craven), 69

Seidl, Ulrich, 4

Seventh Continent, The (1989), 3, 5, 10–22, 24, 25, 39, 46–47, 52, 53, 60, 109, 125, 144; media critique in, 21–22; motif of seeing in, 15–16, 17; motif of viscera in, 18–19, 53

71 Fragments of a Chronology of Chance (1989), 5, 39–51, 52, 53, 139, 154; chance in, 40–41; chronology in, 40; critique of images in, 49–50; media critique in, 48; theme of communication in, 39; use of fragments in, 40, 42–45; use of intertitle in, 40

Sharrett, Christopher, 5

Signs (Shyamalan), 40

Time of the Wolf (2003), 103–13, 148; images in, 105–6, 110; lighting in, 104; media critique in, 103; narrative techniques in, 109; theme of humanism in, 106–7

Waiting for Godot (Beckett), 108

Watts, Naomi, 70

White Ribbon, The (2009), 3–4, 5, 7, 130–36, 156; images in, 131; sociohistorical critique, 135

Zinnemann, Fred, 144–45, 149

Zorn, John, 52, 67, 69

Books in the series Contemporary Film Directors

Peter Brunette is the
Reynolds Professor of
Film Studies and director of
the film studies program
at Wake Forest University.

The University of Illinois Press
is a founding member of the
Association of American University Presses.

Composed in 10/13 New Caledonia
with Helvetica Neue display
by Celia Shapland
at the University of Illinois Press
Manufactured by Cushing-Malloy, Inc.

University of Illinois Press
1325 South Oak Street
Champaign, IL 61820-6903
www.press.uillinois.edu